GRACE

*One Woman's Journey from
Fundamentalism to Failure to Faith*

Marci Preheim
Cruciform Press | March 2014

This book is dedicated to my husband, Arnie,
who, second only to Jesus, is the love of my life.
– Marci Preheim

CruciformPress

CruciformPress.com | info@CruciformPress.com

"I thought this would be a quick read. Ha! I had to stop several times to look up Scripture, ponder, and repent. In *Grace Is Free*, Marci challenges the status quo that we as Christian women don't normally even think to question. She'll step on your toes, but the result will be . . . freedom. If you're like me, you won't even make it to the end of the book before you're sharing it with others."

Paula Hendricks, Marketing Director for TrueWoman, and author of *Confessions of a Boy-Crazy Girl: On Her Journey from Neediness to Freedom*

"I have endorsed very few books, despite a long career with Thomas Nelson. But I enthusiastically recommend Marci Preheim's book, *Grace is Free*, to any woman who has ever suffered under the burden of human expectations for 'how to be godly.' In a simple and conversational way, Marci has skillfully recorded her experiences and advice. These experiences were born as pearls through difficult situations, providing answers that have been tried in the crucible of life. It is a helpful, practical, and down-to-earth book with no fluff. This brand of godliness is one that many Christian men would like to see in their wives."

Charles Z. Moore, former Executive Vice-President, Thomas Nelson, Inc.

"In a time where self-proclaimed spirituality and theologically erroneous Christian hierarchy run rampant, this work could not have come at a better time. Marci punches holes in our thinking and swiftly pulls the rug out from underneath what we define as 'godly.' I have never read a work so inspired, radical, and necessary for this time"

Julianna Zobrist, Christian singer/songwriter and wife of major league baseball player Ben Zobrist.

"Revealing, convicting, and inspiring. What an incredible message of hope for all women striving to be godly! Marci Preheim provides us with a much-needed practical resource for discovering who the truly godly woman is and isn't. Major lies are identified that have held women captive through the years and are replaced with the freedom and truth of God's Word. Here you will find the blending of personal illustrations with biblical insights that reflect her deep commitment to rightly dividing the Word of truth. Marci masterfully reminds women that at the core of godliness is abiding in Christ—in truth, and in faith. This book will be an immeasurable blessing to every woman who seeks to be godly and to be set free at last from the bondage of conformity to rules and standards set by man, not by God. I highly recommend this book and plan to introduce it to others as I share with women in conferences and retreats across the country."

Marlean Felix, Women's Bible Conference Speaker, Elementary School Teacher, Wife of Seminary Professor Paul Felix, and Mother of Wes and Allyson, Gold Medal Olympian 2012.

"As one of Marci's youth pastors, it was both saddening and at the same time incredibly encouraging to read her book. It grieved me deeply to hear how 'law/rules/do-this' Christianity had been communicated and what hypocrisy such distortions of biblical truth created. But to read that through it all, the tenacious pursuing love of Christ was arresting a soul...total delight. Then I let my wife read it. And she was immediately an enthusiastic endorser! Linda said that Marci has written a 'spot-on' work about the unaddressed realities of 'do/don't do' expectations imposed upon women seeking to be truly biblical. She became an instant fan! Marci has obviously identified an 'itch' and provided a timely 'scratcher'! May many women find new freedom to live the biblical Christian life by taking time to seriously consider Marci's excellent work!"

Tom Rempel, Senior Pastor of Faith Bible Church, Lincoln, Nebraska

CruciformPress

Our Books: Short and to the point—about 100 pages.
Clear. Concise. Helpful. Inspiring. Easy to read.
Solid authors. Gospel-focused.

Multiple formats: Print and the three top ebook formats.

Consistent Pricing: Every title the same low price.

Website Discounts:

Print Books (list price $9.99)

1-5 Books	$8.45 each
6-50 Books	$7.45 each
More than 50 Books	$6.45 each

Ebooks (list price $7.50)

Single Ebooks	$5.45 each
Bundles of 7 Ebooks	$35.00
Ebook Distribution Program	6 pricing levels

Subscription Options: If you choose, print books or
ebooks delivered to you on a schedule, at a discount.

Print Book Subscription *(list $9.99)*	$6.49 each
Ebook Subscription *(list $7.50)*	$3.99 each

Grace is Free: One Woman's Journey from Fundamentalism to Failure to Faith

Print / PDF ISBN: 978-1-936760-86-2
ePub ISBN: 978-1-936760-88-6
Mobipocket ISBN: 978-1-936760-87-9

Table of Contents

FOREWORD

The problem with Christian men in the modern evangelical church is that we essentially tolerate their failure to act as men. Not surprisingly, then, the corresponding problem on the other side is the exact opposite—we are largely intolerant of any perceived failure in Christian women.

Our men are in bondage to an extended adolescence that the church has proliferated through low expectations. Our women are in bondage to a form of perfectionism that the church has encouraged through unrealistic expectations. The contrast in what we have come to expect from the genders could not be more stark. The similarity, however, is also stark: the remedy to both extremes is the gospel.

The recent call within evangelicalism for men to quit their negligence has been well and good. There are signs of great progress. The gospel has begun to take center stage, as well as take root in many hearts. Men have been motivated by the spectacle of grace to *take up* their responsibility and lead. But where is the corresponding call on our women to *lay down* the burden of performance set on them by the good intentions of the church? Who is calling our women with equal zeal out of their own peculiar bondage to the same grace of Christ? While setting our men free from one prison, have we abandoned our women to languish in another?

If there is one creature in the church of Christ that silently struggles under the weight of performance more than any other, it may well be the wife and mother. The alchemy for hypocrisy found within her Christian duty is greater than most others. Wives and moms can easily keep the true condition of their hearts from view behind unending tasks and domestic responsibilities. The calls to submission and a quiet spirit may well be interpreted by them as prohibitions against any failure or personal weakness. It's suffocating. Women are expected to have it all together. The end result is mechanical, burdensome, and joyless womanhood which drones on, having forgotten that one thing which rises above all her duties and gives them all meaning—Jesus Christ.

As it is, this burden on Christian women is handed down from generation to generation within the church. Our teaching on womanhood has featured almost nothing of the gospel of grace and has focused nearly exclusively on duty, reducing evangelical Christian womanhood to one extensive and unending "to-do list." This type of Christian womanhood barely rises to the level of a sanctimonious home-economics course.

Thus, almost all of our biblical teaching boils down to a feminized brand of moralism. Most notable is our use of the Proverbs 31 woman as a template for feminine godliness and self-discipline. Without hesitation we assume that this chapter offers a pattern of behavior, and to question this interpretation is sacrilege. Think of all the Christian coffee mugs and Kinkade-like prints that bear this emphasis. The assumption is rampant, but it misses the point. We have taken a beautiful poem composed by a doting husband and turned it into an unbending behavioral strategy for godliness.

In this, and in many other similar ways, we have robbed women within the church of the sincere joy of Christian womanhood. We have kept them back from grace and true freedom. Godliness comes from a relationship with Christ Jesus and a transformed heart, not a list. To be clear, grace does not aim to liberate us from our responsibilities, to excuse neglect, or to deny God's design. But it does aim to liberate us from our tendency to measure ourselves by our performance in fulfilling the duties we are called to do. Our righteousness is outside of us in Christ, not in our relative ability to keep a clean house. It is this latter awareness that liberates us to undertake our duty with complete joy and freedom.

Marci Preheim—believer, wife, mother, servant, friend, congregant and faithful teacher—gets it. By that, I mean she *gets* the gospel of Christ. Having suffered under empty moralism herself and having seen its effects in the lives of others, she was finally liberated by the blinding reality of the grace of God in the cross of Christ. She has in turn made it her mission in life to "free captives" by applying the unending depths of the gospel to the lives of women. Marci's message has sparked a revolution among the ladies in this congregation I pastor. The result has been a true women's-liberation movement. Unlike the ugly outcomes of past movements, the women in this one are not rebelling against the constraints of their God-given roles, but are embracing them in the freedom that can only come from the personal application of the cross of Christ.

Byron Yawn
Senior Pastor, Community Bible Church
Nashville, TN

Introduction
RULES, RULES, RULES

Since the fall, humans have tried to reduce God's requirements of worship, devotion, and loving obedience from the heart to a list of external rules. From Adam and Eve's firstborn son to the present, humanity has wanted to quantify and qualify our relationship with God—to earn his favor, to make ourselves godly. We think that if we have a set of tangible steps, we will be able to follow them. Success can be charted, rewarded, and checked off the list.

The façade of good behavior snares many earnest seekers. What originates as an attempt to become godly ends up quenching the power of the true gospel. In a subtle shift, good things become human obligations—laws the Lord does not require.

The ancient Israelites tried this, adding many more rules to the ones God had given them in the Law and going through the motions of religion. But God was not pleased. He said they drew near to him with their lips, but had hearts far from him (see Isaiah 29:13). The apostle Paul saw the same thing in his day and predicted that it would become more evident in the last days when people will have a form of godliness but deny its power (see 2 Timothy 3:5).

Modern Christians may look down on the Israelites, but this practice is alive and well in Christian circles today. We have a form of godliness but deny its power most of the time. We have learned to hide our sin rather than repent of it. Christians put our own false piety on center stage by forming social groups with each other and isolating ourselves from the world, as though Christianity is primarily about building a safe club for you and others like you.

Christian women do this particularly well. We give each other helpful hints for how to have the perfect quiet time. We share ideas for running our homes efficiently, choosing the best homeschool curriculum, and making discipline charts for children. Christian women (myself included) neglect God's call to live gospel-centered lives in favor of obedience to Emily Post and to each other. It's almost as if obeying rules of etiquette somehow brings us closer to God.

But the more I learn about abiding in Christ, the less I believe that these activities bring me close to God. In fact, they may actually draw me away from him.

It is dangerous to overemphasize behavior. Focusing on behavior leads to external works and a neglect of the heart, which is where true godliness is or isn't. Behavior can be manufactured, but wisdom cannot. When we spend more time trying to appear godly rather than actually being close to God, our motive becomes pleasing people rather than God.

I shared these thoughts with a woman I love and trust.

She is suffering with kidney failure and expects to see Jesus soon.[1] My dear friend confessed that the week prior to my visit she had been too ill to pick up her Bible and have her quiet time. Racked with contrition, she cried to the Lord for forgiveness. The heavy hand of man-made law enslaves those who should be enjoying their freedom and close walk with God. The Bible never gives a regimen for daily quiet time as a requirement for keeping God's favor. Later I wept over the needless guilt she suffered and determined in my heart to expose the legalism that cripples women's souls.

The book you hold in your hands is the product of that resolve.

One
REDEFINING THE GODLY WOMAN

As I look back on my childhood with adult (and regenerate) eyes, I see the false gospel that Christian activity preaches.

In my elementary years I perceived that the more disciplined a woman was, the more godly she was. My Sunday school classes solidified this perception. We were encouraged to keep daily journals, prayer requests, and memory verses on note cards. At the turn of every new year, I resolved to incorporate these activities into my daily life. But I was never able to discipline myself for very long. By the middle of January, I always felt like a complete failure. I asked Jesus to come into my heart several times just in case. But a just-in-case prayer is not a prayer of faith.

During my teen years, our youth group thrived on lectures about the dangers of rock 'n' roll music and premarital sex. We were given charts instructing us on the progression of fornication. We had campfires to burn our sinful music. It always ended with a tearful rendition of "Kumbaya."

As expectations for my behavior grew, my desire to meet them shrank. Many of my friends in youth group partied with the in-crowd at school while maintaining a clean-cut image at church. We had an unspoken code: no one snitches.

Eventually, I lost my desire to keep up appearances. My parents tried desperately to control my behavior and hide it from church people. I was grounded every other weekend. They took my car away and prohibited me from seeing certain friends. My mother stood at the door each evening waiting to smell my fingers to make sure I hadn't been smoking. I learned you don't need fingers to smoke.

My parents tried to preach the Scripture to me, but I didn't want to hear it. It all sounded like a bunch of boring rules. They told me I was risking their positions of leadership at church and that my behavior was hurting them. I didn't want to hurt my parents, but their pleas did not motivate me. I thought: *I'm trying to hide it from you so it won't hurt you.*

I believed that Jesus died on the cross for my sins, and since I had prayed several just-in-case prayers when I was young, I was sure I was saved. I didn't need to fake righteousness the way I thought everyone else in youth group did. My parents were the last to know the real depth of my depravity. They were so blinded by love for me, they couldn't believe their daughter could turn out badly.

At nineteen, I moved to Hollywood. There my lifestyle declined rapidly. I put myself into several situations where God had to supernaturally save my life. However, I did not repent. I pursued my own happiness full-time but still became increasingly depressed and frustrated. Of course, I believed this was everyone else's fault. I decided to go to church to meet some quality people, and I met a young man there who was kind and funny. I pursued him every time I was at church, and we became friends.

One Sunday, he grabbed me by the hand and pulled me across the room where we could talk privately. My heart was in my throat. He looked at me and said "Marci, I'm moving to Hawaii for the next two years for college. I want us to write to each other while I'm gone, okay?" I thought: *This is actually perfect. I have two years to clean myself up.* I made a plan to discipline myself to read the Bible, pray, journal, quit smoking, whatever—very soon. However, I had two years, so I knew there was no real hurry.

We never exchanged letters. A few weeks after his departure, news came that he had been involved in a diving accident. Then, the great blow—he did not survive. As I grieved alone for my friend, my eyes opened, and I finally began to see my sin for what it was. The weight of it was unbearable. Some days I couldn't even get out of bed. I could not figure out why God would take this good man and leave me. I deserved his fate. I had become a hypocrite to impress him. I was the one hiding a mountain of sin, leading a double life.

During a three-month timeframe some dramatic changes took place in my life. I could do little else but read my Bible, weep, and repent. I lost interest in drinking and drugs. I began listening to sermons on tape to satiate my hunger for the Word. I couldn't believe how deeply I had misunderstood the verses I had memorized as a child. My life was apparently changing quickly and obviously: I

didn't notice anything, but people at church and every-
where else did.

Because of my newfound zeal, I lost all my worldly
friends. I even lost most of the friends I had made at
church—you know, the kids in the back row. But that
was okay because I wanted to spend all my time with
people who would teach me the Word. After all those
years of hearing that I needed to "accept Jesus as my
Savior," I realized for the first time that I needed to fall flat
on my face and beg *him* to accept *me* even though I didn't
deserve it. I still had lingering sin, but as the Lord opened
my eyes to it, I realized that I did not have to strive to give
it up—because I hated it. My desires changed daily. The
false gospel of self-discipline I had grown up believing
was now replaced with the true gospel—the gospel of
Jesus Christ who saves sinners.

Those days were lonely but sweet. I felt like it was just
me and God and my sermon tapes. I no longer fit in with
the world, but I didn't quite fit in with church folk either.
Regardless, I attended anything and everything offered at
church.

One weekend, I attended a workshop for women,
expecting encouragement and fellowship. The speaker
started talking about what a godly woman does and
doesn't do, like how a godly woman doesn't chew gum
or skip steps. I looked around to see if anyone else was
as horrified as I was, but everyone seemed to be eating it
up. She talked about memory verse cards and three-ring
binders with prayer requests and how godly it was to rise
early in the morning. At intermission I raced to my car,
tears burning down my cheeks. That old, familiar, false
gospel of Christian activity was like a crushing weight on

my chest. I did not go back to her seminar—I had been saved by the true gospel from my inability to keep all those rules.

Rethinking Proverbs 31

What is the definition of a godly woman anyway? Many people esteem the Proverbs 31 woman as the supreme example. I can almost hear a collective sigh as an unattainable list comprised of early mornings and blistered hands comes to mind. This biblically ideal woman's life has been offered as a template, but does emulating her behavior make women godly?

Imagine with me that somehow the Proverbs 31 woman was here with us today. I'm confident she would reject all the praise about her and give praise to God. She would not point to the things she was able to accomplish in a given day. She would be ashamed of all the fuss we've made over her. She would thank her husband for his encouragement but admit her inadequacies in her next breath. She would not point to herself or anything she has done. She would point to the grace of God found in the righteous sacrifice of Jesus Christ. She would humbly tell us that in spite of her sin and many failures, God has been gracious to her.

Remember, Proverbs 31 does not record this woman's sins and failings, only her victories! So when you and I fail to match her *best* moments at our *every* moment, we are cordially invited to "draw near to the throne of grace, that we may receive mercy and find grace to help in time of need" (Hebrews 4:16).

My whole life I've watched women fall into the same quagmire of conformity. I'm not talking about biblical conformity to the image of Christ, but conformity to an unwritten code of some elusive "godly woman" that doesn't exist. Her dress, behavior, personality, and hobbies are subtly different in each church. But if her behavior becomes a code to live by, then she is a false gospel. This nonexistent woman robs us of intimacy with each other, condemns us as mothers and wives, and holds us in a prison of law that none of us can live up to. She is a form of godliness that denies the power of the true gospel in women's lives. But she is widely preached as the standard of righteousness, which is why the godly woman must be redefined in our generation.

Faith or Formula

The lie that etiquette and self-discipline equal godliness has crept into many churches that are otherwise biblically solid. When I teach this concept to groups of women, I get the same objection all the time: "But Marci, we have to obey!" They think I am teaching that we don't have to obey God, that we should just feel love for Jesus and do whatever we want.

Obedience is not the debate—we all agree that we must obey the Lord. But what exactly should we obey? This has become confusing because people have added their own rules—things God does not require—to the gospel.

All the commands in the New Testament can be reduced down to one: abide in Christ. You won't find many activity-based commands that can be written down on a to-do list and crossed off at the end of the day. The truth is that God is far more interested in our hearts and beliefs than he is in our activities.

Obedience Begins with Belief

Genuine obedience to Christ's commands begins with
belief in Christ himself. Take, for example, the command
to "flee immorality." I knew a woman whom everyone
in the church perceived as godly because she was always
busy with Christian activity. She homeschooled her
children, kept an immaculate house, dressed conserva-
tively, and rarely missed church meetings. Everyone tried
to be like her and felt intimidated by her seeming perfec-
tion. No one suspected this woman was entertaining a
flirtation with a man who was not her husband. One
day, she pulled me aside and confided the allurement to
me. The man was exciting, rich, and full of promises. The
temptation was great.

She had a choice. She could either believe God or her
feelings. God says that immorality is a sin that leads to
death and destruction. Her feelings made her think the relationship would bring exhilaration, happiness, and an escape
from drudgery. If she believed God, she would flee *from*
that illicit relationship *to* God. If she believed her feelings,
she would flee *from* God *to* the relationship. Either way,
her actions would reflect what she truly believed.

Of course, she didn't have to confess the temptation at all. She could have tried to continue that façade of
godliness that everyone else believed. But the Holy Spirit
gave her the courage to be honest with another sister in
Christ and to be honest with her heavenly Father about
what was going on in her heart. Confessing the temptation exposed its foolishness and robbed it of power. She
saw the trap being laid for her, *believed* the allurement
was a lie, *believed* Jesus was enough for her, repented, and
avoided disaster.

Most of us have heard sermons that instruct us to pull ourselves up by our bootstraps (somehow), shape up, and live the Christian life. Those sermons motivate us to obey out of guilt. But on our own we *can't* obey in a way that truly pleases God. The power of God comes from knowing and then believing what is in his Word, for "without faith it is impossible to please him" (Hebrews 11:6). We deny God's power when we claim Christianity but only put on an outward appearance of obedience.

The False Gospel of Christian Activity

When we preach Christian activity more than we preach the gospel, we subtly communicate that God is really only pleased with disciplined people—those who are organized, bright, well-behaved, and particularly well put together—and that there isn't much he can do with weak, unorganized, average people. We communicate that God helps those who help themselves. This message causes people to work on the appearance rather than the reality. It causes people to hide who they really are.

I do not blame the church I was raised in for the fact that I missed the true gospel for so many years. Spiritual things must be spiritually discerned (see 1 Corinthians 2:14). I have no doubt the true gospel was verbally preached to me hundreds of times—yet somehow I came away thinking Christianity is about lists, rules, and social pressure. I believed I needed the "Christian seal of approval" from others in the church.

Recognizing Our Weakness

At the heart of the gospel is a recognition of weakness. The Lord saves both the disciplined and the undisciplined alike—the disciplined from trusting in their capabilities and the undisciplined from their sloth. Older Christians somehow forget their own sinfulness. Younger Christians feel like they will never attain the level of spirituality they see in others. Everyone wants a formula for godly living, but a formula too easily becomes calcified into something that looks like law. To both the disciplined and the undisciplined the Lord says: "Come to me, all who labor and are heavy laden, and I will give you rest.... For my yoke is easy, and my burden is light" (Matthew 11:28, 30).

This simple gospel is a gift given to those who *believe* in the finished work of Jesus Christ on the cross and his resurrection—not our own righteousness. Abiding in Christ is not only the secret to being used by God; it is knowing his joy more fully. It sets us free to focus on *one purifying ambition* rather than on a list of rules. That one purifying ambition is to draw near to the Savior. It is basking in the freedom of what he has already accomplished for us. Abiding in Christ is the key to our purpose in life, to lasting joy and godly relationships. It's the good news for believers.

Making It Stick

- The word *abide* means to stay in a given place, state, relation or expectancy—to continue, dwell, endure, be present, remain, stand, or tarry. The promise to the one who abides in Christ is that Christ will also abide in her (see John 15:4). What do you think Jesus means by this? Is abiding in Christ an inward reality or an outward work? Do any of these potential definitions even remotely resemble a to-do list?

- For further study, read Galatians 3:1–5 to see Paul's response to the Galatians who had fallen into this trap. Have you found yourself caught up in following rules that have nothing to do with obedience to Christ? Give some thought to when and how you began believing you should follow those rules. Think about what it would be like to be free from social pressure and follow Christ by faith instead.

Two
EXPOSING THE STEPFORD WIVES OF EVAN-GELICALISM

In *The Stepford Wives* (first a 1972 novel and later a movie—twice), a society of men find a way to transform their wives into the women they always thought they wanted: beautiful and thin, finely dressed, domestic goddesses, and tigers in the bedroom. These wives have no opinions, and they answer "yes, dear" to whatever their husbands ask. The men love it…for a while. But what they discover over time is the dissatisfaction of fake relationships based only on externals. In the story, husbands turn their wives into robots. In the church, women do it to each other.

As a new believer, I could not get enough of God's Word. I listened to sermons every day on my way to and from work. At home, I plopped down on my room-mate's bed, and we would talk about all we were learning. Scripture poured into me and out of me. Then a girl from our church asked us to join her for a Bible study. On the first morning, she gave us our assignments, a schedule, and a strict order to be on time. She put herself in authority and made sure we complied with the rules. She rebuked us when we didn't follow through "excellently." My roommate and I started feeling trapped. The motivation shifted from joyful conversation about the Lord to reports on how well *we* were disciplining ourselves to please her. That study lasted about three weeks.

The Scriptures call upon older women to teach younger women what is good (Titus 2:3–5). It goes on to give a list of "good" things to teach. But in that list of six things, only one is an activity—"to be busy at home." Even that is vague and differs in practicality for each individual. The other five are heart issues: love, self-control, purity, kindness, and submission.

You can be busy at home with lots of good things: homeschooling, crafts, nutrition, home decorating, sewing, housekeeping, couponing, and so on. Are these what the apostle Paul had in mind when he said "teach what is good"? These things can all be good—unless they become the standard for what a godly woman does. We fall short in our calling to teach each other when we only define *good* in domestic and external terms. If a woman's heart isn't an overflow of the gospel, even her best domestic efforts cannot make her godly.

We don't like messy people we can't fix. Our solution is to come up with a code of behavior we can live by and enforce on others. Our motivation is guilt and the fear of man's (or woman's) disapproval. We give them rules to follow and schedules to keep. The one who will not (or cannot) follow the code is met with disapproval when she fails. She may be told to "do better" and sent on her way. This unfortunate disciple may then merely pretend to follow the code, hiding her failure—thus, a hypocrite is born. This is how the church loses her first love. No one is motivated long-term by guilt. Guilt may reach the behavior, but it will never reach the heart.

The Pharisees were guilty of an extreme form of this type of rulemaking. They added more laws to God's law in order to *appear* more holy to people. Jesus said to them, "Woe to you, scribes and Pharisees, hypocrites.... [who] appear righteous to others, but within you are full of hypocrisy and lawlessness" (Matthew 23:27–28). Their self-righteousness blinded them to their need for a Savior. Jesus asked them, "How can you believe, when you receive glory from one another and do not seek the glory that comes from the only God?" (John 5:44). Here we are two thousand years later doing the very same thing.

Depending on Christ's righteousness is the joyful alternative to human achievement. The beauty of the gospel is realized when we humbly admit we have nothing to offer—no righteousness to bring. Christian women know this but don't always live it in front of each other. Instead, we try to prove the opposite. Covering our sin and wearing a mask of external righteousness, we fool others into thinking we are godly.

We were not called to be robots. Jesus said in John 13:34–35, "A new commandment I give to you, that you love one another: just as I have loved you, you also are to love one another. By this all people will know that you are my disciples, if you have love for one another." I cannot truly love someone if I am enslaved to her opinion of me. Being fake is not love.

Abiding in the Vine

We don't demonstrate our love for Christ and others by adhering to a list of rules but by abiding in him. Understanding what it means to abide in Christ is so important that it was the subject of Christ's parting words to his disciples. He gave them a word-picture that they could remember through the crisis of his death. In John 15:1-5, he spoke of the dependence of branches to their vine:

> I am the true vine, and my Father is the vinedresser. Every branch in me that does not bear fruit he takes away, and every branch that does bear fruit he prunes, that it may bear more fruit. Already you are clean because of the word that I have spoken to you. Abide in me, and I in you. As the branch cannot bear fruit by itself, unless it abides in the vine, neither can you, unless you abide in me. I am the vine; you are the branches. Whoever abides in me and I in him, he it is that bears much fruit, for apart from me you can do nothing.

This analogy gives one requirement for fruitfulness: to abide or remain in the vine. As living branches we passively receive everything—salvation, faith, discernment, forgiveness, a righteousness from God (Romans 3:21). Indeed, "His divine power has granted to us all things that pertain to life and godliness, through the knowledge of him who called us to his own glory and excellence" (2 Peter 1:3). What else could we possibly need to do but abide in him?

The single command to the living branches is to stay connected to the vine. Translation to believers? Continue to believe Christ by faith no matter what happens. "The

righteous will live by faith" (Romans 1:17) not by sight.
Your faith will be proven through various trials (1 Peter
1:6–7), so we should not be surprised when they come
(1 Peter 4:12). Surely Peter never forgot Jesus' words on
the night he was arrested: "I am telling you now, before it
takes place, that when it does take place you will believe
that I am he" (John 13:19). Peter knew that when we
undergo trouble, we generally prefer to escape or fix
things on our own rather than rest in our Savior and
wait on him. That's why we need to understand this vine
imagery that Jesus gives us.

God the Father is the gardener. He is intimately
involved not only in the fruit-bearing process but in the
relationship of each branch to the vine. He removes the
dead branches, and he cuts away the worthless parts of
the living ones. Pruning can be painful, yet it is an essential
part of God's continual care over our lives. Romans 8:28
teaches us that God works through our circumstances,
even the painful (pruning) ones: "And we know that for
those who love God all things work for good, for those
who are called according to his purpose."

Therefore, even seemingly unhappy things that come
our way are good things—even if they *feel* bad. As our
circumstances collide with our biblical knowledge, we
learn to grab hold of Christ in faith. Through difficult
times, our faith will be strengthened as we believe his
Word and stand firm in Christ's strength.

My Weakness, His Strength

To abide in Christ's strength, we must continually be
aware of our weakness. In order to trust in God's strength,
we must discredit our own. The two cannot exist together.

About eighteen months after my conversion I met "Nora," a chaplain at a women's prison. I was mesmerized by her stories and asked how I could serve with her. I just wanted to be with her. She told me I could join the team from the church that visited the prison once a month. I signed up the first chance I got.

The team consisted of three people: the teacher, the song leader, and me. I did nothing but observe the first few times. After that, I served in small ways. Once, I read a verse from the Bible. Another time, I shared a brief testimony. It was a simple service that included the three of us, Nora, and one hundred prisoners.

One day on the way back from the prison, the woman who always taught the lesson told me she would be stepping away from the ministry. I looked at her with horror. "Who is going to teach the prisoners?" I asked.

"You are," she said.

I didn't know you could say no to stuff like that back then. I was twenty-two years old and scared to death. I felt the weight of the ministry bear down on my shoulders. I cried to the Lord and panicked for a whole month. I cried more. I paced. I prayed. I searched my Bible. I scribbled some notes. I cried some more.

When I went to the prison the next time, I shared the gospel in all its beautiful simplicity. The response was powerful. That was my first taste of the Lord's power in my weakness. I went back regularly and had the same result each time. I shared whatever I was learning at the time. Then I met my husband, married, moved to a new city, and left that ministry to another terrified newcomer.

The Lord planted a seed of desire in me—a desire to return to that kind of powerful ministry. In my new city, surrounded by all new people, I knew God was calling me to be a Bible teacher, but no one else did. As I spent time thinking of the days at the prison, a new seed began to grow in my heart—a seed of pride.

I forgot the crying and the praying and the weakness. I began to think it was my giftedness—rather than the power of the gospel—which had brought about that response. Surely if these people had seen me in action at the prison, they would want me to teach here. They would at least want my input and wisdom in conducting the various ministries at church. I believed I had the gift of discernment. But what I called the gift of discernment was really a critical spirit, a lack of submission, and pride.

The Lord did not give me a platform for teaching right away. He put me in charge of the church nursery and the preschool departments. We know we need God's help with some activities, but others we think we can manage ourselves. The nursery? How hard could it be? Get volunteers, make a schedule, and call people to remind them—easy. But no one wanted to volunteer. People didn't show up for their scheduled time. And when I called with reminders, I got excuses for why they needed to be removed from the schedule.

I missed the church service almost every Sunday and continually fought feelings of bitterness. Not only was I taking care of my own babies every day, but I went to church and had to take care of everyone else's too—it wasn't fair.

One day, I'd had enough. I called everyone I could think of, seeking volunteers. Every person said no. I was angry and judgmental. I cried out to the Lord. I said, "What else can I do, Lord? I've tried everything."

I suddenly remembered the lesson I had learned at the prison but didn't (until then) think applied to the nursery: God was waiting for me to recognize my weakness before intervening with his strength. In that moment, my perspective changed and a burden was lifted. After all, the Lord wasn't asking me to put my head on a chopping block. He was only asking me to serve the children and their parents for a couple of hours a week.

Having found some peace after my little fit at the foot of the cross, I got up and folded laundry. I thought about a conversation I'd had earlier with my friend Sarah. *Hey, I haven't called Sarah*, I thought. *I wonder if she would be willing*. I called. She and her husband happily agreed to serve.

My approach changed from that moment on. Rather than calling people to guilt them into service, I began to pray that the Lord would lay the need on people's hearts and bring them to me. And if there was a slot I couldn't fill, I knew he was calling me to fill it. He often made me wait until the last minute, but my striving ceased, and my faith grew. I lived in the book of Isaiah: "In returning and rest, you shall be saved; in quietness and in trust shall be your strength.... Therefore the LORD waits to be gracious to you, and therefore he exalts himself to show mercy to you. For the LORD is a God of justice; blessed are all those who wait for him" (Isaiah 30:15, 18).

No matter how gifted we are, the Lord wants us to be mindful of our weakness. The same Lord who fueled my gospel presentation to one hundred prisoners is also the One who lifted my preschool burden. I learned again to seek him with all my heart and to be a servant leader. I couldn't take credit for any success—I was dependent on the Lord for everything.

Desperation Versus Discipline

Honestly, abiding in Christ comes more naturally to us living branches when we are suffering. Then no one needs to teach us how. We cling to him out of sheer necessity. This is how he teaches us that he can be trusted. This is how our faith is proven. This is where humility is born. If we can learn how to abide in Christ from our times of suffering, then we learn to lean on him even during times of ease.

The entire Trinity is at work in our lives if we are living branches. The Father will prune away all that is worthless and orchestrate our circumstances for spiritual growth. The Son has paid the price for our sins, which allows us to be living branches on his vine. He is now interceding on our behalf at the right hand of the Father. The Holy Spirit dwells within us as the nourishing sap, compelling us to draw near to Christ.

Fruitfulness comes from *believing* more, not necessarily *doing* more. As we abide in Christ, fruit is naturally produced. In nature, branches do not strive to produce fruit. As long as the branch is attached to the vine, it *will* bear fruit. Remember: "Whoever abides in me and I in him, *he it is that bears much fruit*" (John 15:5). There are no added conditions.

What Should I Do?

Christians are always wondering what to *do*. I get nervous when I hear people talk about methods for spiritual growth, because that is God's work, not ours. People have been trying to *make* themselves righteous for centuries. The human heart craves law. It wants *steps* so righteousness can be measured. It will try to find every loophole so sin will still fit into the picture. It justifies anger and self-righteousness. But our inability to keep the law is what we were saved from! Paul wrote, "Are you so foolish? Having begun by the Spirit, are you now being perfected by the flesh?" (Galatians 3:3).

If we teach people that it's only acceptable to spend time with the Lord early in the morning, we alienate all the people who enjoy him at night. Why would we declare every other time of the day ungodly? Rather than spending time with the Lord during her children's nap time, some young mother may give up altogether because she failed to get up early. We've lowered the standard of "pray without ceasing" to "pray at five o'clock in the morning."

Bible reading and prayer are important in the believer's life, but what is the motive? Is it discipline for discipline's sake, or is it longing to know Christ? Is it something we should do that we feel guilty about or do we *believe* it is the source of power, encouragement, comfort, and strength that we desperately need? Do we evangelize out of guilt? Why do we journal or memorize scripture or attend Bible studies? Are we pleasing men or God? The means so easily become the end.

It is by God's grace that any of us hunger and thirst for his righteousness. Desperation draws us to desire him. If we must discipline ourselves against our will to draw near to the Lord, then there is a bigger problem than lack of discipline. There's a crisis of faith. There's an arrogance that *believes* there's no urgent need for his power. *Thanks for saving me; I've got it from here, Lord.*

As we draw near to Christ *he* bears the fruit through us. We can dream big as we think about how we would like to participate in the kingdom of God, but we have to let the Lord put us there. We often go to one extreme or another. Either we think we can't do anything for God (let alone "great things") because we evaluate our limitations, or we think too highly of ourselves and try to serve God in our flesh. Neither can bring about fruitfulness: it comes only from God's power working supernaturally in us.

A Body, Not a Business

The body of Christ is not a corporation. We don't all follow the same path, beginning in the mailroom and retiring fifty years later as honored leaders. Each of us is uniquely gifted at the moment of conversion. Each believer follows an individual path that has been laid out in advance (Ephesians 2:10) for a specific purpose—to glorify God.

There is no place for selfish ambition in the church. We don't decide what we will do for God or what our gifts will be. Hard work does not guarantee a position in leadership, nor does a life of strict discipline always yield greater usefulness. Obedience from anything other than faith is legalism. It will not produce fruit that will last (John 15:16). It will not persevere. It will not save. "For whatever does not proceed from faith is sin" (Romans 14:23). When the gospel ceases to be pure and central, the church loses her first love and her power.

I put my testimony in this book to reveal the power of the gospel as it is administered through human weakness—both to save and to sanctify. But I have the same story as innumerable others who supposedly came to Christ as children (with just-in-case prayers), walked away as teens, and finally came to believe in the true gospel of grace alone, through faith alone, in Christ alone. If you too have such a story, perhaps it's time to share it with others around you.

Making It Stick

- It's important for women to have friendships across many generations; each has something to offer the other, as Paul noted in his letter to Titus. If you are an older woman, is there a younger woman within your purview to whom you might open your heart? Try to let your relationships unfold naturally. Remember, there are no rules!

- Learning to welcome adversity seems counterintuitive, yet the power in suffering lies in the *belief* that God is doing something good even if it doesn't *feel* good. What good things have come from adversity in your life? What do Romans 5:1–5 and 8:18–25 reveal about our hope through suffering?

- Do you evaluate your limitations and feel disqualified for service or do you feel like you have to be in control because no one will be able to meet your standards? Think about which extreme most describes you. Most of us have struggled at one time or another with both.

Three
WILL THE REAL EVILDOER PLEASE STAND UP?

When did it become okay for Christians to be angry people? As our culture declines, the anger of religious people seems to grow. Sin is discussed more openly these days, and we have to warn our kids about it. How dare the world be so worldly! We try to get people to conform to our Christian standards, but they won't cooperate. We are angry that those sinners are ruining our perfect Christian utopia.

Around the time I started doing a little more public speaking, my mom visited. We talked about my tumultuous teenage years and all that she and my dad had gone through then. She knew I had been sharing my testimony and felt like she of all people should know my story. I didn't think she would be able to handle it. But she insisted, so I shared a few stories. Sure enough, she got mad at me as if I had done those things the day before: "Marci, how could you? I never did any of those things when I was your age. It wasn't socially acceptable."

I understand my mom's fear and worry about what could have happened, and I know her love for me fuels those protective feelings. I did do a lot of stupid things. My mom didn't know the Lord in her teens, but she was motivated by social standards. She doesn't understand why I couldn't just behave like she did.

I challenged her by asking, "Do we preach a gospel of social pressure that forces certain behavior, or do we preach the good news about a Savior—Jesus Christ—who died and rose again to reconcile sinful people to God?" After a thousand conversations, my mom is getting to the place where she understands that I *had* to fall that far in order to look up and see the gospel that saves *sinners*—not people who think they are good enough.

There's a dire problem with thinking that you are good enough—it's not just a minor glitch in self-assessment. The problem is that you deceive yourself into thinking that you don't really need the gospel as it is. The problem is that you don't really know the Lord and will, in the end, be cast away from him. We learn this in one of the most frightening passages in the Bible:

> Not everyone who says to me, "Lord, Lord," will enter the kingdom of heaven, but the one who does the will of my Father who is in heaven. On that day, many will say to me "Lord, Lord, did we not prophesy in your name, and cast out demons in your name, and do many mighty works in your name?" And then will I declare to them, "I never knew you; depart from me, you workers of lawlessness!" (Matthew 7:21–23)

Those *workers of lawlessness*, or *evildoers* in other translations, are religious people. They put their faith in Christian activity (even done in Jesus's name) but missed the Christian faith altogether. The scariest thing this passage reveals is the prevalence of self-deception: *many* will call Jesus *Lord* but not know him. It is possible to believe you are a Christian because of your Christian activity yet *not* to be a Christian! Can you imagine a more horrifying discovery than to stand before the gates of heaven fully expecting to go in but instead being turned away for eternity?

The biggest danger of self-deception is that no one believes herself capable of it. And so the deception continues. If questions arise in her heart, she deceives herself into thinking no investigation is necessary (2 Corinthians 13:5). Perhaps she believes the lie that Christian activity validates faith. Or maybe she mistakenly equates biblical knowledge with godliness. God is not pleased with knowledge or activity if it is coupled with spiritual pride. He gives his grace to the humble (James 4:6, 1 Peter 5:5).

In the Bible, the first self-righteous angry person shows up in Genesis 4. Cain was religious, which meant that he became angry when God accepted Abel's sacrifice but not his. He wanted to bring the fruit of *his* labor for God's approval rather than bring what God required—a sacrificial lamb.

When I was a new convert, I met another repentant sinner at Bible study. He and I stood out in that clean-cut group of people—traces of our past still showed in our appearance. "Jerry" had been involved in a homosexual lifestyle and had contracted AIDS, which back then meant he wasn't going to live very long. The reality that he would stand before Jesus soon brought him to repentance and therefore to Bible study. He wanted to grow close to God with the time he had left. After a while, though, Jerry stopped attending Bible study and eventually left our church altogether. I heard that as he neared death, he turned to the homosexual community for compassion, having found none at church.

The human heart tends to compare the self with others. It is easy to look at someone else and think he is getting what he deserves while we ignore the reality of what we deserve. We become so accustomed to God's grace that we feel entitled to it. We think we have earned it by our "good behavior," so others must earn our compassion by *their* good behavior. Jesus knew people like that:

> He also told this parable to some who trusted in themselves that they were righteous, and treated others with contempt: "Two men went up into the temple to pray, one a Pharisee and the other a tax collector. The Pharisee, standing by himself, prayed thus: 'God, I thank you that I am not like other men, extortioners, unjust, adulterers, or even like this tax collector. I fast twice a week; I give tithes of all that I get.' But the tax collector, standing far off, would not even lift up his eyes to heaven, but beat his breast and said, 'God, be merciful to me, a sinner!' I tell you, this man went down to his house justified, rather than the other. For everyone who exalts himself will be humbled, but the one who humbles himself will be exalted." (Luke 18:9–14)

This tax collector understood something the Pharisee did not—the magnitude of his sin and therefore his need for a savior. Self-righteousness blinded this Pharisee to the fact that he, like the tax collector, had a mountain of sin. Social pressure may have kept him from acting upon what was in his heart, but that didn't mean he was innocent. If he had understood that sin goes deeper than activity, he would have huddled in the corner and begged for forgiveness too.

Growing up, I encountered many angry people who admonished me to stop my bad behavior. But I don't recall anyone ever telling me I couldn't. Some Christians wore their anger as a badge, smiling smugly after they had bulldozed someone into proper behavior.

Maybe we have forgotten Paul's description of love in 1 Corinthians 13: "Love is *patient* and *kind*" (verse 4). His description of what love *isn't* is even more incriminating: "Love does not envy or boast; it is not arrogant or rude. It does not insist on its own way; it is not irritable or resentful; it does not rejoice at wrongdoing" (verses 4–6). Controlling someone with anger may successfully change her behavior for a while, but it will never reach her heart. Likewise, parents who dominate their children with anger may succeed in getting them to comply, but over time their hearts will become embittered. They will only comply until they find a way to escape.

Let's Force Them into Faith

Sometimes we view evangelism in a rather unloving way. We have adopted the idea that if Christians can talk louder and be more obnoxious than the culture, people will listen and repent. Maybe we can force them to see things our way. My definition of a good evangelist used to be someone who was brave enough to corner some unsuspecting non-Christian until she mumbled something resembling a sinner's prayer. I remember watching this take place as a kid and hearing people comment how bold so-and-so was with the gospel. My concern here is not with motivation, but technique and approach—not the *why* of evangelism, but the *how*. Evangelism must begin with love or it is worthless (1 Corinthians 13:1–3).

When I was pregnant with my first child, I went to a birthing class, and the best thing to come out of that class was a lifelong friend. "Elizabeth" and I became close a couple of months after our children were born, after I ran into her at Walmart. We *oooh*ed and *ahhhh*ed over each other's infants for a while, and then Elizabeth looked at me and blurted out: "I need a friend. Here's my number—can we get together?" Her eyes filled with tears as she told me that her husband traveled for his work and she was lonely.

I took this as a sign from God that I was to evangelize her. She moved to the top of my prayer list and became "my project." Elizabeth and I did a lot together. She called me to go out to breakfast, to go shopping—she even called when she was on her way to the grocery store just to see if I wanted to tag along. Every time we got together I determined to turn the conversation to the gospel.

But Elizabeth is a master of subject-changing. We would get to the gospel every now and then, but we would never park there for long. One day, I decided I was just going to *make* it happen. I didn't care what direction the conversation went, I was going to get back to the gospel. We ordered some cheap Chinese food at the mall and sat at a small table in the food court. Breaking open my egg roll, I started in on my rehearsed speech: "Elizabeth, if you were to die tonight…"

Just then, a woman with a tray full of Chinese food tripped by our table. Food went flying, and the woman seemed hurt. I was annoyed. I just knew Satan was nearby sticking his foot out to distract the gospel. I had Elizabeth's full attention, but my five-step gospel presentation was thwarted again.

Elizabeth jumped from her chair. "Oh you poor thing! Are you okay?" she asked, running to the lady's side. Only then did I think I should help too. To my shame, I don't even remember what happened to the woman who fell. I only remember my frustration at not being able to share the gospel with Elizabeth.

As time went on, I grew to love Elizabeth. She came to church with me often. I gave up on giving her the canned presentation I had planned that day but continued to pray for her and looked for opportunities to talk to her about the Lord. Mostly, those opportunities came as I just shared my life with her.

Of all of my adult days on this earth, there is one that stands out as sacred, and it happened unplanned despite all of my earnest attempts to evangelize my friend. Elizabeth had found out her husband had become involved with another woman on a business trip, and this woman was shameless. She began stalking and harassing Elizabeth, confronting her in public places and causing her to fear going out. Finally, the courts had to get involved, and Elizabeth and her husband had to pay a humongous sum of money to make this woman go away.

During that season, I spent more time with Elizabeth than ever before. She wanted me to read Scripture to her so she could get her mind off her fear and rage. I bumbled around reading a psalm here and a proverb there. For the first time in my life, I was at a loss for words. Elizabeth had always said she would leave her husband if she ever caught him cheating. Since she was so hurt and angry, I could not imagine things going any other way. After some counseling with an older couple in our church, however, Elizabeth decided to forgive her husband. To say you forgive someone is one thing—to be able to do it is another. Nowhere in Scripture will you find a tidy set of steps on how to actually forgive someone in your heart. That's because ultimately you cannot do it; Christ must do it through you.

One day, Elizabeth's husband called and asked me to come over. Elizabeth was screaming and throwing things, and he was worried about what the children were hearing. I didn't want to go. What could I say? How did I know I wouldn't be that angry in her shoes? What more Scripture could I read to her? But I went. By the time I got there, she was in her bedroom hiding under her covers. I felt so weak and helpless, but I went back there and got in on the other side of the bed. We just lay there. She sobbed silently.

Finally, I laid my hand on her arm and started praying. Then I turned to her and said, "I think you should pray." I had never heard Elizabeth pray, but she started whispering some semblance of a prayer. What came next was nothing less than supernatural. There in the dark, Elizabeth, for whom I had been praying forever, began repenting of her *own* sin. Her husband's sin had brought her unconscionable pain, but she didn't even bring that up. The Holy Spirit's presence in that room made me tremble so violently I hoped she wasn't distracted by it. It was almost as if the curtain was pulled back a little so I could see the bloodied battlefield of good and evil fighting for my friend's soul.

She was changed after that night, and so was I. All my striving and scheming to manipulate my friend into saying some contrived prayer seemed so foolish. What I thought was Satan hindering my gospel presentation I now know was God—holding my tongue until he had prepared the soil of her heart to receive the seed of the gospel. The difference in this form of evangelism from all the "programs" I have learned about is *love*. I had earned the right to share the gospel with Elizabeth in her darkest hour because *she knew I loved her*, and even though I did so poorly, the Lord revealed himself to her.

If we focused on abiding in Christ, he would give us his love for others. We wouldn't waste our time trying to come up with clever speeches and manipulative methods. Our mode of evangelism would change. Our idea of who is and who isn't a good evangelist would change, and every believer would be empowered with what *should* fuel the gospel—love.

Gospel-Centered Programs or Program-Centered Gospel?

We Christians so easily lose sight of our first love and become preoccupied with programs. When this happens the gospel can die off in one generation. Take the early days of the Ephesian church as an example. Their story is a lesson for what can happen in individual families as well.

The people in the Ephesian church had been radically saved out of witchcraft and goddess worship. Ephesus was a hub of temple prostitution. The temple to Diana (also known as Artemis) was one of the Seven Wonders of the World. She was a goddess of fertility, and worship of her centered on sexual extremes and drunken revelry.

The first Christians in Ephesus were so zealous for the gospel that they burned their sorcery books in the public square. This act was not only a bold proclamation of their faith but a serious financial sacrifice. They didn't care. They had been set free from the bondage of their sin. Their love for Christ burned brightly—literally. They knew the depth of their depravity and therefore understood the depth of forgiveness and grace they had received.

Over time, they became the most well-taught church in the entire region. How ironic, then, that only a couple of decades after the book-burning, Jesus himself said he appreciated all their hard work but they had lost their first love (Revelation 2:1–7). They had busied themselves so much with Christian activity that no one noticed when the power of the Holy Spirit slipped out the back door.

When we lose our first love—which is Christ—our primary love becomes *ourselves*. The people in the Ephesian church had lost sight of what they had been saved from (v 5). They did good works and held high moral standards (vv 2–3), but the gospel gets lost when the focus becomes making people behave.

Christians make this same mistake in parenting. Raising children with the idea that they can make themselves righteous if they only have good rules for behavior kills the gospel that clearly proclaims the opposite. It is a subtle shift with deadly consequences. The purpose of the law is not to make children righteous but to reveal sin and lead them to Christ (see Romans 7:7–8, Galatians 3:19–24).

Returning to Your First Love

The Lord gave three instructions to this congregation who had lost their first love: remember, repent, and return.

The first instruction was to "remember...from where you have fallen" (Revelation 2:5). The Ephesian church originated with folks who knew their capacity for sin. As their behavior changed, so did their memory of their depravity. We are all depraved. The Bible says: "None is righteous, no, not one" (Romans 3:10).

The second command was to repent. Repentance is the cure for pride, which is the root of all other sin. Our society (and even our churches) trains us to cope rather than repent. Rather than repenting of anger, we justify it, entertain it, blame it on others, and end up passing it on to our kids. We distract ourselves with diversions and coping mechanisms.

I used to vacuum when I was struggling with anger. Vacuuming my house made me feel like I was putting something in order—even if every other area of my life was in disarray. The angst I felt was my unwillingness to surrender my situation to God and humble myself before him. I wanted to figure out a solution rather than wait upon him. I have learned when I am struggling with these feelings to leave my vacuum in the closet and repent of my sin so the Lord can take it away, "casting all [my] anxiety on him, because he cares for [me]" (1 Peter 5:7). I am either abiding in Christ or trying to control. By God's grace, I am vacuuming less and learning to abide instead.

The final command was return. The concept of *returning* is implied in the words "do the works you did at first" (Revelation 2:5). The interesting thing about this command is that these Ephesian believers were "doing" all sorts of things (vv 2–3). What had changed was their motivation (v 4). This happens so easily in the church. We so often stop being motivated by love for Christ and become motivated by something else, like maybe guilt from other people. Therefore, Christ called the Ephesians to humble themselves, repent, and return to love so radical it was willing to burn its sin in the public square.

Making It Stick

- What makes you angry? What does anger *not* bring about, according to James 1:19–21? Are you tempted to control other people with anger? What is the result? How do you react to people who try to control you with anger? If your reaction is compliance on the outside, what is your internal reaction?

- What is your method of evangelism? Do you feel guilt for not sharing the gospel more often? Do you think guilt is a good motivation for evangelism? How do you think drawing near to the Savior could motivate you to be a better evangelist while at the same time setting you free from scheming and striving to make sure God saves your loved ones?

Four
SIN
MANAGEMENT

One Sunday morning when I was working in the church nursery, I took a moment between welcoming newcomers and signing children in to scan the sanctuary from the nursery's half-door. My eyes rested on a face I hadn't seen in many years. I called out to her joyfully, "Leslie!"

I riffled through my memories to the last time I'd seen her. "Leslie" and I grew up in the same church. We spent a lot of time together in our teenage years. We rebelled together and then lost touch when I moved to California. I was shocked to see her in church now, and I knew she would be shocked to see me.

She hadn't noticed me yet. I started biting on my cuticles (a nervous habit of mine since youth), realizing what her presence in my church could mean. You can hide a lot of sin by moving away and starting over. I had shared my testimony with many people at church, but here was a witness. Details of my sinful past were at her disposal. When I finally got her attention, we shared a surprised and then hesitant smile—both of our minds filing through memories we might rather forget. I could tell she had the same thoughts I had. She was happy to see me, curious about how I made it back to church, and hoping that I wouldn't tell people what I knew about her.

When you do not have the power of the Holy Spirit working within you, sin management is all you have. Sin management is putting up a good moral front and managing your sin by hiding it from people rather than confessing it to the Lord. Growing up, Leslie and I loved our sin. We didn't want to give it up. We learned to manage it with external goodness and to keep it from those who demanded good behavior. But sin management only works as long as you can keep it hidden. Neither Leslie nor I was ever very good at hiding sin. I thank God for that. If I was able to hide my sin, I might still be enslaved to it, just as the Bible tells us.

> And this is the judgment: the light has come into the world, and people loved darkness rather than the light because their works were evil. For everyone who does wicked things hates the light and does not come to the light, lest his works should be exposed. But whoever does what is true comes to the light, so that it may be clearly seen that his works have been carried out in God. (John 3:19–21)

Since that first meeting at church, Leslie and I have had many lunches. We have compared stories about the years we were apart and how the Lord brought us each to repentance. She and I still sit for hours and sort through the false gospel we both believed growing up. We marvel at God's graciousness to draw both of us separately to himself and then bring us back together. We wonder about our peers who were able to hide what we could not. Did they ever come to understand the true gospel, or are they still striving under the bondage of sin management?

Both Leslie and I default to a "striving" mode when we are not consciously believing the true gospel. It's in our DNA to feel like we are not praying hard enough, reading enough Scripture, or doing enough godly things to deserve God's favor. We fall into the mentality that somehow with Christian activity we can draw down God's favor upon us. Believing we have his favor no matter how we perform in a given day is the hardest thing for us to do.

Devotion, Desire, and Dependence

It's dangerous to discuss the "how to" of abiding in Christ because we may be tempted to get out pens and paper and make a list of activities *we think* will make us godly. We need to remind ourselves that abiding is a heart issue, not an activity. Don't get me wrong. True faith does result in acts of righteousness. But righteous works apart from faith are worthless before God. No one seeks God naturally (see Romans 3:11). The desire (the *want*) and the ability (the *how*) to abide come from him: "for it is God who works in you, both *to will and to work* for his good pleasure" (Philippians 2:13).

Faith is invisible. Jesus compares it to the wind (see John 3:8). Only the effects of faith can be seen by others. However, since these effects can be fabricated to impress others, I must evaluate my genuineness. Here are some illustrations that help me determine if I am abiding in

Christ or deceiving myself with Christian activity. Maybe these three descriptions will be helpful to you. They are devotion, desire, and dependence.

Devotion

One way to understand true devotion is to think about romance. In the first few months of young love, devotion comes easily. The heart consumed with adoration naturally performs acts of affection. We think about that special person 24/7, and we dream of ways to show our love outwardly.

I find another simple illustration of devotion when I look at my dog. She is so devoted to me that when she is locked out of the room, she cries at the door until I let her in. The first thing she does in the morning is come to my side of the bed and jump up so she can catch a glimpse of me. Whether I have been gone five minutes or five hours, I get the same enthusiastic welcome from her when I walk in the door. She did not require lessons in devotion. No one taught her how or when to do it. But my dog is utterly devoted to me.

These illustrations probably are not foreign to you. Most of us know what devotion is. Why, then, when we talk about "doing our devotions," do images of dry reading and empty prayers come to mind? The Lord wants us to be devoted to him from the heart. True acts of devotion originate there. When Jesus tells us to "seek first the kingdom of God, and his righteousness, and all these things shall be added to you" (Matthew 6:33), he is talking about our heart's desires.

God calls us to seek him first. We have all heard sermons on rising early to have our "quiet time" to start our day off right. But what he is telling us here has nothing to do with chronological time. He wants us to seek him *first* as a *priority*. Each of us makes time for what is really important to us. Jeremiah 29:13 says, "You will seek me and find me, when you seek me with all your heart."

Devotion is not something we can muster up. When we don't feel devoted, we can confess that and ask the Lord to give us a more devoted heart. And he will. I remind myself that the Bible calls us wandering sheep for a reason. Even when we have enjoyed blessing after blessing because of close fellowship with the Lord, we tend to forget and wander back to our own selfish goals. What we are devoted to gets our time and energy. Examining those two things is a good place to begin a personal appraisal of faith.

Desire

If it sounds like I have mastered the devotion part of abiding in Christ, I need to confess something. There are times I find myself not caring about fruitfulness. I lose my desire to stay close to Christ; I selfishly want to pursue my own agenda and fleshly desires. I go through the motions of prayer or Bible study with the idea of crossing it off my list so I can get back to doing my own thing. As time goes on, my heart begins to harden to the things of God, and I start to act out what has collected in my heart instead — whether that's anger, ungratefulness, selfishness, or something else.

When a desire for Christ wanes, our behavior reveals it. If those behaviors remain unchecked, they lead to bondage. Some people, like me, give in to selfish anger. For some, it shows up as paralyzing fear; some grow increasingly depressed and lazy, living in denial of their sin. Drunkenness or other escape methods may follow. These are the manifestations of heart issues that we have become very good at hiding from others. So ask yourself what you desire. Psalm 37:4 says, "Delight yourself in the LORD, and he will give you the desires of your heart." But this verse does not mean that God will fulfill our selfish desires and instantly give us a new Corvette or a winning lottery ticket. Instead, it means that as we delight in him, he will give us *new* desires, ones that will lead us closer to him.

The longer we walk with the Lord, the more our desires change, usually without even realizing it. I experienced something similar in my marriage. When my husband and I were first married, we looked forward to Thursday nights because we would throw together a simple dinner and settle in for an evening of "must-see TV." After we had children, our schedule got busier, and must-see TV evolved into "must get some sleep." One day, I was flipping through the channels and landed on a rerun of one of our favorite shows from years before. But I could hardly stand to watch it. The jokes were vulgar, and the characters' lifestyles mocked the devastating results of sin that I had watched play out in the lives of real people. I was no longer entertained by it—on the contrary, it grieved me.

If someone had told me early in my marriage that it was not godly to watch that TV show, I would have smugly defended myself by claiming Christian freedom. I would have resented the rule being placed on me and probably would have desired to watch it even more. But over time, without my realizing it, the Lord changed my desires. A supernatural change in desire is much more powerful to change behavior than the rules we give each other.

As we live by the Spirit, we are no longer under the law, gritting our teeth while trying to obey a bunch of rules. When we abide in Christ, we will be supernaturally transformed over time and experience a greater desire to live in obedience to the Lord. We will be motivated by joy, not guilt. "For this is the love of God, that we keep his commandments. And his commandments are not burdensome. For everyone who has been born of God overcomes the world. And this is the victory that has overcome the world—our faith" (1 John 5:3–4).

Dependence

Although I hate to admit it, I have a big mouth. When I am not living by the Spirit, everyone knows it. I have learned I need the Lord to temper my tongue so I am useful to him. Otherwise I can tear down the kingdom with that little member of my body. I often pray that the Lord would put a gate over my mouth and give me discretion not to say everything I think. I get into even more trouble when I try to be the center of attention or make people laugh. This weakness reminds me that if I am not abiding in Christ, I can hurt others and wreak havoc with my tongue. I don't want to act this way, but apart from abiding in Christ, this is who I am.

I depend on the Lord to change me from the inside. In the South, they have a saying: "Whatever is in the well comes up in the bucket." It's clearly a takeoff on Matthew 15:18, in which Jesus says: "But what comes out of the mouth proceeds from the heart, and this defiles a person."

This tells me that my mouth is not the problem at all — it's my heart. Apart from Christ, my heart is unclean or defiled.

Abiding in Christ requires a constant awareness of how much we need the Lord. We learn to trust in his righteousness and not our own. We utterly depend on him to show us how to be useful, and being useful to the Lord becomes the believer's greatest joy. This also means depending upon him in our relationships with others.

Colossians 3:12–17 lays out how we are to treat one another, but those verses make it clear that we cannot accomplish any of these actions or attitudes in our own strength. To live out godly relationships, we must depend on the power of the Spirit. Unfortunately, we often try to *be* the Holy Spirit for others, trying to control and motivate others with harsh words, coldness of heart, or with judgmental accusations.

As a new convert I began attending a Friday night Bible study. I was late each week because I had to shower before the study. I didn't want anyone to know that I was a smoker, a residual of the party life I had left behind. Someone pulled me aside and said it wasn't honoring to the Lord for me to be late every week.

I thought, *If you only knew how really sinful I am, you would think nothing of tardiness.* If she had taken the time to wonder if I had a reason to be late, she would have approached me in a different way. I had plenty of things to feel guilty about, so being shamed for being unpunctual was not the kind of help I needed. In the weeks that followed, I avoided her out of fear that she would discover some of my more notable sins. Thankfully, I was so hungry and thirsty for truth that I didn't let my discomfort keep me from coming to hear God's Word each week—late or not.

Jesus and Women

Jesus has a different message for women than we have for each other—a message of mercy and grace. Look through the gospels at the narratives of his encounters with women: not once does he applaud a woman for her domestic skills. On several occasions, however, he commends women with great faith and reckless love. One word captures these women—humility. They approached him needy and desperate, aware of their unworthiness. He granted their requests for mercy. He welcomed their worship. Many of them became his close friends.

A third character is present in most of the accounts of Jesus with women. This character takes different forms but is always the same—angry and judgmental. It may be a group of annoyed disciples begging Jesus to send away a nagging Canaanite woman, or a self-righteous Pharisee who thinks, "If this man were a prophet, he would know who and what sort of woman this is who is touching him, for she is a sinner" (Luke 7:39). Once it was a crowd of bloodthirsty men with stones waiting to blame their brutality on a woman caught in adultery on Christ. There is even a sister, a fellow worshiper of Christ, tattling because her sister is not *doing* what is expected of her.

You know the story. Martha was busy serving and Mary was sitting at Jesus' feet. Often when this story is taught there is a disclaimer. It goes something like this: "Well, Mary should help her sister, but in this case she chose what was better," or "I'll tell you what, I'd rather stay at Martha's house." We feel for Martha. We've been where Martha has been. But that disclaimer never shows up in the Bible. This reveals our natural pull to focus on *doing* instead of *believing*. We secretly side with Martha and want to learn that later Mary helped her. But it's not there. Pay attention to what Jesus said: "Martha, Martha, you are anxious and troubled about many things, but *one thing is necessary*. Mary has chosen the good portion, which will not be taken away from her" (Luke 10:41–42).

People naturally react with anger when they perceive a lack of respect for "the rules." Yet the *one thing necessary* is to draw near to Christ. The rest of our lives should flow from that one pursuit. Martha ignored Christ to focus on things that didn't matter.

We do this too. For example, between seminars at a women's event, I found myself in a conversation about the gospel and realized I was speaking with someone who desperately needed to hear it. She and I stayed outside of the seminar. Five minutes into our conversation, someone poked her head out to warn me that I was missing the talk on how to set a fabulous table. I assured her that I would come in a minute. Five minutes later, she poked her head out again: "Marci, you're missing it!" I wanted to say, "No, *you're* missing it!"

We get the gospel wrong so often. Believers tend to think it is only for the salvation of unbelievers. We rarely reflect on our own need for its power in daily life and miss opportunities because we're so distracted with externals. The true gospel sets women free to abandon worldly ideals and draw near to Christ. His standard is actually much higher than outward performance: it is inward devotion, desire, and dependence. Through freedom and grace received from him, we are able to give others freedom and grace rather than try to control them. We are free to be emotional with Jesus (yes, you read right). We are free to have transparent friendships and to dialogue without fear of judgment. When we admit weakness rather than cover it, we will be more useful to the kingdom than we've ever been.

Making It Stick

- For discussion: Abiding in Christ is about understanding what it truly means to trust Christ with every aspect of your life. The Lord is working in each of us to stir desire, motivate devotion, and cause us to depend upon him. This will look different for each one of us depending on our personalities, our spiritual gifts, and our season of life. How can you know if you are abiding in Christ? What is your cue that you are not abiding (i.e., anger, fear, dissatisfaction, restlessness, a loss of peace)?

- The devoted dog crying outside the closed door illustrates devotion to Christ. Think about times you have cried out to God. How was the door opened? How does the psalmist cry out to God in Psalm 86? How is this similar to ways you have cried out to God? What truths about God does the psalmist recall for comfort?

Five

STANDING FIRM

A young girl was saved out of a world of sin. She had been heavily involved in drugs, drinking, and promiscuity. She was grateful to be saved and set free from her bondage to wickedness but was still drawn to a man from her past. He was her first love—if you could call it that. Years before, she had lost her virginity to him in what amounted to date rape. Nonetheless, he had a hold on her. They had an on-again, off-again relationship. When she came to Christ it had been off for a while. Sure enough, only a few short weeks into her newfound faith, guess who showed up on her doorstep?

She invited him in, believing she was strong enough in her faith to witness to him. Maybe the Lord would save him and they could be happy together in a new context. It was a trap she did not see coming. She was too weak to resist his advances. She gave in to temptation and he stayed with her all weekend.

For weeks afterward, she was tormented by guilt and accusations from the enemy: "You will never be a Christian! Look how weak you are! The Lord does not want you now! What if someone at church finds out? You might as well go back to your old life—that is *who* you are." She did end the relationship for good, but instead of repenting and believing Christ paid for that sin, she tried to forget it, work harder, and do more Christian things to offset the guilt.

So often, Christians try to fight the enemy with religious activity. Yet the Bible does not recommend activity as a solution to our problems. It assumes that the day of evil will come and says that when it does, we must put on God's armor and stand firm (see Ephesians 6:13). Being aware of the spiritual war is our first line of defense. And if we understand how the enemy operates, we will have more success in thwarting his plan (see 2 Corinthians 2:11). If Satan's one objective is to get you to fall, then your one objective is to stand.

Many Christians believe it is God's grace that saved them, but they then believe the lie that they must be "good" to remain in his favor. They don't understand they have inherited *his* righteousness (Romans 3:21–22). We fall short when we try to be good because it is the power of his Word and the Holy Spirit that changes us, not our own ability. As we grow in knowledge and love for the Savior, our behavior will begin to change. In his book *Abide in Christ*, Andrew Murray points out the error of those who don't understand that weakness and failure are actually the conduits of abiding.

> The idea they have of grace is this: that their conversion and pardon are God's work but that now, in gratitude to God, it is their work to live as Christians and follow Jesus. There is always the thought of a work that has to be done, and even though they pray for help, still the work is theirs. They fail continually and become hopeless, and the despondency only

increases the helplessness. No, wandering one; as it was Jesus who drew you when he spoke, "*Come*" (Matthew 11:28), so it is Jesus who keeps you when He said, "*Abide*" (John 15:4). The grace to come and the grace to abide alike are from him alone.[2]

Suffering and failure reveal who we are and who we put our trust in—ourselves or God. They show us our need for God when we have exhausted all our human effort and wisdom. It is still painful to go through trials even when trusting God through them. But there is peace in the knowledge that: "after you have suffered a little while, the God of all grace, who has called you to his eternal glory in Christ, will himself restore, confirm, strengthen, and establish you" (1 Peter 5:10).

Eliphaz, Bildad, and Zophar Got It Wrong!

People suffer. And when they do, Satan loves to add guilt to their grief. Just think about how much unwanted advice flows from the mouths of well-meaning people to others in difficult circumstances. We learn what *not* to do from Job's friends. The Lord told Eliphaz, "My anger burns against you and against your two friends, for you have not spoken of me what is right, as my servant Job has" (Job 42:7). What exactly had Eliphaz and his friends said? They offered trite advice based on poor assumptions they made about Job and his situation. They meant well but spoke lies.

Platitudes spoken to someone in pain are as unwelcome and awkward as an uninvited drunk at a party. Assumptions are painful to bear. Requiring a suffering person to follow rules for "suffering well" is not only anti-gospel, it is cruel. The body of Christ was meant to comfort the suffering saint, but sometimes we get it way wrong.

The wife of a youth pastor carried her baby full term, safely delivered him, and enjoyed snuggling him for one day at home. The next day, speeding back to the hospital, he breathed his last, leaving her to reconcile how this could have happened. She reached out to the church. The leadership officially informed her that she must joyfully accept this as God's will for her life. Then they handed her a gift certificate for a free turkey.

The day after the funeral, the women's ministry leaders met. It was business as usual, checking items off the agenda. She was present in body only. She could feel her body preparing to feed a baby that was no longer in her arms. Her thoughts went back to the day prior. As she had laid her hand on his tiny casket, all she could think about was the gaze of those around her—those who would hold her accountable to keep her emotions in check. Over the next few months, people showed up—not with food, gifts, or encouragement but with exhortation. She need not spend her days mourning. That would not be pleasing to the Lord, they said. She dutifully held back her tears, believing the lie that the Lord would be displeased if she shed even one.

More than a decade later, the tears flowed freely as she recounted these events to me. I could not imagine where this teaching came from or who would have the audacity to enforce it. Jesus did not forbid grief. He never turned away a woman for being emotional. On the contrary, he himself wept on several occasions—most notably at Lazarus' tomb. Coldness is never appropriate in the body of Christ, nor will it will motivate anyone to practice Christ-like behavior. It is a lie to say that joyful suffering means keeping a stiff upper lip and painting on a smile. That only adds hundreds of pounds to the burdens that suffering people already carry. There is such a thing as joyful suffering, but it is based on the knowledge that someday God will wipe every tear away. Until then, joy and tears often go together.

Divide and Conquer

Suffering softens some hearts and hardens others. I saw this starkly one afternoon while eating lunch with two ladies, one of whom was my good friend while the other was a new acquaintance. The latter began openly sharing her discontentment with her marriage, and I could not help but feel compassion. But to my surprise, she began comparing her unhappy marriage with my seemingly happy one. I asked how she knew I had a happy marriage, and she stated some assumptions based on what we looked like on Sunday mornings. I told her that I had my share of struggles in marriage as well, but she dismissed them as small based on what she had observed.

She then proceeded to compare her marriage with that of the other woman present. My eyes met my friend's and then dropped to my salad, for just two years prior, I had walked with this friend through a severe crisis in her marriage. She had found great freedom and victory on the other side of that painful trial, but to correct this woman's wrong assumptions would have required telling her much more than she needed to know.

Our lunch partner assumed that we did not understand her pain and therefore could not judge the actions she planned to take. In her mind, we could not present her

with truth because we could not understand the depth of
the temptation she felt. She believed that her marriage was
beyond repair and that she was the only one who suffered
this way. She was so focused on escaping her suffering that
she could not see what good things could have come from
it. She was determined to "take over from here."

I did not see her much after that lunch. She eventually disappeared from our fellowship. Once we isolate
ourselves, the enemy will be right there to overtake us
with lies we willingly believe.

What this woman did not know (or want to believe)
is that even though my friend and I may not have experienced her precise trials, we could still relate. Whether or
not we can understand someone else's specific struggles,
we all understand temptation. James describes temptation
in hunting terms: we are enticed by sin just as an animal
is enticed by bait, and as soon as we grab hold of it, we
are dragged away to our death, like an animal caught in
a trap (James 1:14–15). The woman at lunch was eyeing
some bait that my friend and I had in some form also been
tempted by. She could not resist the enemy's lies about her
own circumstance or about our experiences. We tried to
warn her that it was a trap, but she was blinded by the bait.

Where's My Happily Ever After?

One of Satan's most successful schemes is to convince
us there is something or someone who will bring us
our "happily ever after" here on earth. C. S. Lewis put it
this way in his book *Mere Christianity*: "If I find within
myself a desire which no experience in this world can
satisfy, then the most probable explanation is that I was
made for another world."[3]

No person or material thing has ever brought us lasting happiness, so why do we continue to believe that something or someone will? The whole of creation is groaning under the curse that leads to this frustrating search for ultimate satisfaction—especially believers.

> And not only the creation, but we ourselves, who have the firstfruits of the Spirit, groan inwardly as we wait eagerly for our adoption as sons, the redemption of our bodies. For in this hope we were saved. Now hope that is seen is not hope. For who hopes for what he sees? But if we hope for what we do not see, we wait for it with patience. (Romans 8:23–25)

Many women seem to have an unwritten list of things they think will make them happy. Walt Disney told us that once Prince Charming came along, we would live happily ever after, and many of us believed him. A baby was usually next on the list. Perhaps attaining money, living in a beautifully decorated home, wearing designer clothes, or having friends in certain social circles became part of that happiness list. Every woman's list would be somewhat different but also very much like others. But whatever we think will make us happy—apart from Christ—is a lie. It is idolatry. Any one of these things can bring temporary joy, but when it becomes our number-one pursuit, it becomes an idol that brings only disappointment and disillusionment. But take hope. The frustration we experience because we cannot live happily ever after on this earth is meant to fuel our hope for eternity.

Although the ultimate spiritual war has been won at the cross, we still face daily battles while we wait for our eternal rescue. The only way to stop believing lies and start believing truth is to be transformed by the renewing of our minds (Romans 12:2). That means getting the Word of God in our heads however we can. We can't believe Christ or abide in him if we don't know what his Scripture says.

As a young mother of two active children, I found it difficult to sit down and read anything. I would fall asleep in minutes from exhaustion. So I became dependent on Bible teachers on the radio to feed me scriptural truths. I learned to plan my day around my favorite teachers, folding laundry at ten-thirty and cleaning house at two o'clock. These teachers, along with my pastor on Sunday mornings, spoke truth into my life so my mind wouldn't be idle to entertain lies. After all, it is hard to believe the Lord will use you for anything when you spend all day washing clothes and cleaning up toys. But God used those moments during those years to store up his truth in my heart.

None of the biblical writers laid out Bible-reading plans or memorization schedules or formulas for prayer. The reality is that spiritual disciplines will play out very differently for different people in different stages of life. Instead, the biblical writers call us to a higher standard than merely a disciplined life: to love God's Word, believe it, hide it in our hearts, and pray without ceasing.

The Power of Prayer

A group of women from my church conduct a monthly chapel service at a mission for women recovering from addiction. After many years, our program is well organized. It is easy to put our faith in our well-run program and forget the true source of our power.

Recently, we began to recognize hardness in the

hearts of many we ministered to. It became difficult to communicate and build relationships with them. At the same time, one of the newer women from our church, "Lydia," confided that she felt guilty going with us because she didn't feel she had anything to offer. She just wanted to come to hear the teaching and enjoy the fellowship. She was intimidated by the rough lifestyles of the mission women. Convicted about her feelings, Lydia committed to pray daily for one of the women at the mission, but she didn't telling anyone else that she had begun doing this.

The next month, we faced the same disappointing hardness of heart in everyone—except one woman. Lydia sat next to the woman she had been praying for and simply asked her, "How are you?" Without knowing Lydia had prayed for her all month, the woman began to open up. Lydia gave her some simple counsel, prayed with her, and found herself overjoyed at how God used her even though she felt she was weak. The newest believer among us shamed us by her childlike faith and her willingness to be used through prayer.

Those who believe in the power of prayer pray. If you don't pray, it is not because you are not disciplined enough but because you don't really *believe* in the power of prayer. We prove by our prayerless lives that we believe more in our human ingenuity than in God. Just as a human relationship grows closer by time spent together communicating, so does our relationship with God. He is not as concerned with how or when we pray as much as whether or not we *pray*. We don't have to worry about our prayers being eloquent or modeled after someone else. Instead, we need to depend on our God: "The Spirit helps us in our weakness. For we do not know what to pray for as we ought, but the Spirit himself intercedes for us with groanings too deep for words" (Romans 8:26).

We may be overwhelmed at the thought of fighting a war (especially with an unseen enemy) until we realize that we are merely called to stand (Ephesians 6:11). Actively believing the truth protects us from falling. Our behavior will follow our belief. When the dust clears and we look up, we will see that Christ fought the war for us. All we did was believe him. It is our faith that shields us from the enemy's fiery darts.

Making It Stick

- How does the enemy trip you up? Does he keep you busy with the unimportant, causing you to disregard your priorities? In what ways are you a perfectionist? If you can't arrange the "perfect quiet time," do you avoid spending *any* time with the Lord? Has Satan deceived you into believing in a "happily ever after" on earth? Who or what do you not have now that you think would bring you satisfaction if you could just attain it?

- Women especially tend to hold themselves to high standards of behavior. Maybe you learned to "put on a happy face," which can be good advice since petty complaints can take on lives of their own when we focus on them. But in times of sorrow, keeping a stiff upper lip seems unbearable. Even Jesus wept. Think about how to be authentic about grief — your own and that of others. The apostle Paul did not hide his grief. Read 2 Corinthians 1:3–11 and observe his openness about how he even "despaired of life itself." What good things came because of his grief (vv 4, 6, 9–11)?

Six
A POWERFULLY MUNDANE LIFE

Brother Lawrence, a seventeenth-century monk, was clumsy and crippled from a war injury and admitted he could not do anything well. He worked for the first half of his adult life in the kitchen of a monastery and the second half in the sandal shop. His days were consumed with washing dishes and fixing other men's used sandals. He died unaware of the impact his life would have on thousands of people — even several hundred years later.

During his life he wrote letters to friends explaining the joy he and others had in their relationship with Christ. He found that being mindful of the Lord's presence and thinking about the truth of Scripture — even during the busiest times of the day — brought supernatural peace and joy.

Brother Lawrence's small circle of friends was so affected by his life and testimony. They felt he had a secret that needed to be shared with the world, so after his death, they compiled their letters from him. The end result was a little book called *The Practice of the Presence of God*. The following is an excerpt:

God has many ways of drawing us to Himself. He sometimes seems to hide Himself from us. But faith alone ought to be our support. Faith is the foundation of our confidence. We must put all our faith in God. He will not fail us in time of need. I do not know how God will dispose of me, but I am always happy. All the world suffers and I, who deserve the severest discipline, feel joys so continual and great that I can scarcely contain them. I would willingly ask God for a part of your sufferings.

I know my weakness is so great that, if He left me one moment to myself, I would be the most wretched man alive. Yet, I do not know how He could leave me alone….Let us always be with Him. Let us live and die in His presence. Do pray for me, and I pray for you.[4]

Brother Lawrence never claimed to be a theologian, but what he discovered here was profound, even as it was also no real secret. What he "discovered" was the power of abiding in faith. He experienced the mighty power of the gospel through his weakness. He did not take on the establishment. He simply understood his weakness and believed in the sufficiency of God's grace and forgiveness. This man who spent his life as a common worker made a big difference in the world simply by abiding in Christ and doing what he found in front of him to do.

Over the years, I have observed Christians immerse themselves in all sorts of causes. During my childhood, many Christians signed up to sell products through a multilevel marketing company—they all became very passionate about soap. But even good causes can distract

us from the gospel. Politics, the environment, public
health issues, homeschooling, vegetarian eating (or any
other kind of special diet), exercise—the list seems endless.
While many of these are good causes, Christians are
neither commanded in Scripture to participate in them
nor forbidden from doing so. Instead, what seems clear
is this: if we do participate in such activities, we must not
put our faith in them or allow them to take center stage
in our lives. Christians often use Scripture to back such
endeavors, but these external things do not draw us near
to God (see 1 Corinthians 8:8).

When Christians get distracted with "good things,"
they often end up losing their passion for the gospel,
which is the power of God unto salvation (Romans
1:16). I know someone who became so passionate
about homeopathic healing that she talked about it with
everyone she encountered. She used to be that bold
with the gospel. All of her energy turned from rescuing
people's souls to rescuing their temporal bodies.

Guilt or Grace

Hebrews 13:9 says, "It is good for our hearts to be
strengthened by grace," but we are more often motivated
by guilt than we are by grace. Most sermons have one
of two objectives: 1) to motivate people with guilt to
do something, or 2) to motivate people with truth to
believe something. Every preacher desires to motivate his
audience, and guilt is a powerful tool to motivate behavior
changes in the short term.

Truth is an even more powerful tool, though. Truth
motivates belief, which then motivates behavior changes
in the long term. Jesus offers to take away our guilt, setting

us free from its bondage. The hardest part is admitting our guilt and *believing* he will take it away. Instead, we try to cover it and vow to *do* better next time. We need a steady diet of the truth about God's grace.

A woman in the church called me one Sunday afternoon. She was wrestling with some of the same struggles I had early in my Christian walk and was seeking some accountability. She asked if I would meet with her regularly to help her avoid falling back into old patterns. It's a good thing that she did not initiate this conversation with me a few years ago. I might have set up weekly meetings and given her a checklist of duties to monitor her growth. How arrogant of me to think I could control someone else's spiritual growth with rules! I can't even discipline myself.

Instead, I told her I had a joyful message for her. Over coffee the next day, I explained that we all fear falling back into old patterns. Our human tendency is to find a tangible priest, put laws in place, and vow to never allow this. But trying to add rules and masters to the gospel doesn't transform hearts. I don't have the power to keep her from falling, but I could speak truth to her. After being saved supernaturally by the grace of our Lord Jesus Christ, do we doubt his ability to finish the job? Must we take over from here?

Again, the gospel comes to our rescue and frees us from these entanglements. We remember to believe in the power of Jesus to transform us—not in ourselves or any other human agent. "He who began a good work in you will bring it to completion at the day of Jesus Christ" (Philippians 1:6). The Bible reminds us that we depend completely on our Savior.

I encouraged my new friend to let our relationship (and others) develop naturally. I warned her not to put her faith in me or any other "mentor" but to cling instead to Christ. Because our struggles were similar, we could warn each other of the dangers of believing Satan's lies. We could remind each other about finding strength in the truth of God's Word. We could pray for each other. We could encourage others in the church to engage in friendships and, ultimately, true fellowship, like this. And although we realize that our struggle is not yet over, we can hope together in the time when it will be.

All true believers will someday stand shoulder to shoulder at the throne of grace. In that day, we will see how weak and prideful we were on this earth. No one will foolishly compare herself to the person standing next to her. No one will gather followers to himself. We will be too consumed with Christ. In that day, we will all marvel at his grace and wonder that he saved such wretched, sinful, undeserving people like us.

What's Your Something?

What does it mean in practical terms to live by faith and not by sight (2 Corinthians 5:7)? We were all born with an instinctive desire to put our faith in something we believe will bring satisfaction. All our hopes and dreams are centered on that something. When sin entered the scene in Genesis 3, mankind abandoned pursuit of God for the desires of the flesh. If we were honest with ourselves, even believers would have to admit that our "something" is not always God. Our earthly "somethings" often change as they disappoint us one by one.

To live by faith means our "something" is Christ. To

live by faith means we believe that he himself, not what he can give us, is our reward (Genesis 15:1). Like he did with Abraham, God reveals himself to us. Our job is to believe him. When Abraham simply believed the Lord, "he counted it to him as righteousness" (Genesis 15:6).

If we are truthful we find that most things we want to put our faith in are tangible (marriage, job, children, friendship, health, money, status). Many of these are "good things" but they will never satisfy our deepest longings. They are not our ultimate reward.

Whatever our "something" is, it can become an idol that consumes our thoughts. Our thoughts motivate our activities. If our "something" is money, then our thoughts will revolve around creative ways to make it, spend it, invest it, and so on. If it is marriage or children, then we may conduct our relationships according to what we believe works, rather than what God says. Even religious activity can become an idol if pursued for selfish reasons, such as to please people or gain recognition.

We like formulas and guarantees: if I do X, then I will receive Y. We like to feel we are in control of our own happiness. I have sat with many disillusioned women who have fallen into this trap of entitlement. They believe if they behave a certain way, then God owes them earthly blessing. They tell me they have done everything right and cannot understand why they haven't received their blessing from God. This prideful attitude displays a misunderstanding of God's grace. We must return to Abraham's posture toward the unseen God:

> What then shall we say was gained by Abraham, our
> forefather according to the flesh? For if Abraham

was justified by works, he has something to boast
about, but not before God.…Now to the one who
works, his wages are not counted as a gift but as his
due. And to the man who does not work but believes
in him who justifies the ungodly, his faith is counted
as righteousness. (Romans 4:1–2, 4–5)

God does not negotiate. He won't be manipulated
into giving us what we want by our seemingly good
behavior. He owes no one. Everything he does is for our
good and his glory—even if it doesn't *feel* good.

Red Spots

I woke up one morning in May 2006 to find my hands
covered in red spots. I thought I'd had an allergic reaction
to lotion or soap because the rash ended abruptly at my
wrist. I wasn't concerned. But when I pulled the covers
back, a tide of fear swept over me as I saw red spots also
covered my feet, ending abruptly at my ankles.

Perhaps it was natural to go immediately into denial.
Surely it was just a freak allergy and nothing to worry
about. So I let it go until I could no longer ignore it. The
rash began to morph. The red spots turned into purple
welts and spread to meet each other. I knew I had to take
action when a store clerk looked at the money I was
handing her, recoiled with a little gasp, and looked at me
like I was a leper.

Over the next few months I was given test after test
by various doctors. At any given time, I had a Band-Aid
with a big piece of cotton under it somewhere on my
body. The word *lupus* was thrown around more than
any other. One doctor said, "I'm sure you have lupus,

but don't go home and Google it." So the first thing I
did when I got home was Google it! Another seed of fear
took root as I looked at pictures of worst-case scenarios
and read about impending kidney failure. I turned my
computer off, realizing I should have obeyed my doctor,
and ran frantically to God's Word. Hebrews 12 came alive
to me during that time:

> It is for discipline that you have to endure. God is
> treating you as sons. For what son is there whom
> his father does not discipline?…For [our fathers]
> disciplined us for a short time as it seemed best to
> them, but he disciplines us for our good, that we
> may share his holiness. For the moment all discipline
> seems painful rather than pleasant, but later it yields
> the peaceful fruit of righteousness to those who have
> been trained by it. (Hebrews 12:7, 10–11)

My faith was tested by this ugly rash. My vanity was
exposed, as I feared it would spread to my face or cause
my hair to fall out. Every difficult relationship, every
deficiency in my character, and every priority was put
into perspective during that time. I spent a lot of time
repenting. In a weird way, I felt privileged to have the
Lord working so personally on me. When I drew near to
him, he drew very near to me. I had unexplainable peace—
until I ventured out in public.

One of the most oppressive parts of that trial was
that I was bombarded, even by Christians, with remedies
for healing myself. I was exhorted to "take control of my
health." I gave in a few times and spent many hours online
researching diets and products people insisted would heal

me. Every time I gave in to the pressure to look into these remedies, I came away feeling overwhelmed, panicked, and confused. When I drew near to Christ, on the other hand, I found peace.

There was freedom in relinquishing control of my body to my heavenly Father. Even if my kidneys were to shut down, as frightening as that would be, I knew I was in his care. That is not to say I did nothing to care for my body, but I ultimately learned through that terrifying trial to abide in faith—not to abide in self-saving. The opposite of faith is fear, a highly contagious virus that spreads rapidly and easily paralyzes its victims. The anti-fear serum is faith in God. He doesn't want us to waste time worrying about our physical bodies (Matthew 6:25). It requires faith to believe his promise that he will give us exactly what we need, when we need it.

At present, this confusing illness has not given me too much grief. The Lord has given it to me as a gift to train me to abide in faith. Every now and then it shows up in some strange symptom that serves to remind me that my body is in the Lord's hands. It reminds me of my mortality and what I want to do with the time I have—mainly, to pass on the true gospel to my kids and other people he has placed in my life.

Making It Stick

- Our first instinct is to react to any stressful situation by doing something about it. Psalm 46:10 reminds us to "Be still, and know that I am God." How do you handle stressful situations? How can believing God's Word help you process difficult circumstances?

- God doesn't bargain with behavior. As much as we would like to make deals with him—*I'll be good, Lord, and you'll give me my reward*—he does not work like that. He won't be manipulated into fulfilling our fleshly desires. Instead, meditate on passages like Romans 8:1–6. What is true of the mind controlled by the Spirit (v 6)?

Seven

KEEPING YOUR EYES ON CHRIST IN THE STORM

Sometimes, even grown-ups need pictures to understand concepts. Perhaps the most vivid illustration of abiding in faith is found in Matthew 14. Here we find Jesus's disciples fighting a tempest in the middle of the sea when Jesus came to them walking on the water. Peter called out: "Lord if it's you, command me to come to you on the water." Jesus said, "Come" and Peter jumped out of the boat (see v 28).

It must have been exhilarating to walk on the sea as if it were a wet sidewalk. Peter lived above his circumstances (literally) for a few minutes until something distracted him. He took his eyes off Jesus and began to look instead at the wind and the waves. He traded faith for fear and began to sink.

Peter had enough faith to get him out of the boat but not enough to keep him on top of the water: as soon as he took his eyes off Jesus and put them on his circumstances, Peter started to doubt whether Jesus was in control and could continue to sustain him. In that moment, Peter believed his circumstances were bigger than his God. Even while Jesus was proving that he could be trusted, Peter began to doubt.

The Wind and Waves of Female Relationships

I am part of a small committee of women who direct the women's ministries at our church, which is often a joy but sometimes a challenge. A few years back a woman who was a very strong leader began attending our church. I liked "Sandra," as she was a say-it-like-it-is kind of person. We became friends, and she joined our leadership committee, but over time, it became clear that her philosophy of ministry was different from ours. We tried to be good listeners, give her the freedom to express her views, and then talk about them without anger. Our lone request was that she discuss these differences only with the leadership so we could sort them out privately and prevent division in the body.

Before long I began to hear that Sandra was slandering us. She started her own group of ladies who met together, instead of going to the Bible study at our church, and I began receiving phone calls from confused ladies who expressed doubts about the legitimacy of our ministry. This was a difficult situation, of course. After careful questioning, I was usually able to determine that Sandra had planted these seeds of doubt.

Betrayal from an enemy is one thing, but betrayal from someone you thought was your friend is downright painful. I did not react well to this attack on my character or our ministry. I looked around at the storm brewing all around me, and I feared the waves. Sandra even convinced some of our Bible study leaders that we should spend more time teaching domestic skills and less time in the Bible together. I was tempted to pick up the phone and build my own army against her. I lost my temper several times when I heard about the poison she was spreading. It seemed that her full-time job was to bring our women's ministry down.

I spent a lot of time wrestling with the Lord about this, asking him why he would allow such opposition. I specifically fretted over how to repair my reputation. Basically, I wasted a lot of time trying to keep myself on top of the water instead of putting my eyes on Christ and letting him handle Sandra.

I now see that Sandra's presence in our church drew me and other leaders closer to the Lord. I finally sought his wisdom when I had no more of my own, realizing that I could not control her with anger or kindness or anything else. I could not control who would follow her and who would recognize how dangerous she was. The only thing I could do was put my eyes on Jesus and resist falling into the same trap Sandra had. My tongue could be just as deadly as hers. I could kill the gospel by focusing on stopping her. In my heart, I handed her over to the Lord to take care of, confessed my prideful anger, and became free. I learned to *do* less and *believe* more.

In the same way that resistance and pain strengthen our muscles, trials and opposition strengthen our faith. For example, I hate to exercise. I would rather curl up with a book and a cup of coffee any day. I force myself to exercise, however, because my body needs resistance training so that it will be strong and able to handle the demands of my busy life. Still, every time I'm on the elliptical, I count the minutes until I can get off—keeping in mind the benefits I will enjoy from it if I persevere.

So it was with my relationship with Sandra—and with Christ. It takes resistance to make things stronger. The Lord is the perfect trainer. He applies just the right amount of resistance to our lives that will drive us to him. He knows how much we can handle and when it is time to rest (1 Peter 5:10). He also promises never to leave or forsake us, and he offers his wisdom so we can endure the pain with the right perspective.

The opposition I faced from someone else's slander brought *my* sin to the surface so I could see it and repent. It humbled me and caused me to draw near to Christ. It caused a longing in my heart for Christ. It made me willing to be the janitor in the kingdom if that's what he was calling me to. The women's leadership team learned to seek better communication and protection from the elders of our church, which resulted in greater unity.

Ultimately, Sandra left our congregation. When it became clear that she had moved on, one of the committee members said to me: "Are you glad she's gone?" I said: "No, because there will be ten more just like her." In Acts 20:30, Paul warned the Ephesians that "from among your own selves will arise men speaking twisted things, to draw away the disciples after them." I should've expected it and kept my eyes on Christ from the start.

The Storm That Stretches Faith

Just as I wondered why the Lord would allow such opposition in his church, we may ask why Jesus would send his disciples out alone into a storm he knew was approaching.

Why would he allow them to fear for their lives all night and not come to their rescue until morning? When Jesus finally did come, he knew exactly where to find them on that vast sea. He must have known their plight all along. Could there have been a good reason for them to suffer this hardship?

This incident took place immediately after Jesus had fed five thousand men plus their wives and children with just a few loaves and fish. The Gospel of Mark gives insight into the disciples' hearts when they got into the boat that evening: "they did not understand about the loaves, but their hearts were hardened" (Mark 6:52).

Jesus had a purpose in waiting to rescue his disciples. It was to soften their hearts so he could manifest his glory to them. A hard heart can never see God's glory. So God often allows struggles in our lives to soften our hearts, rid us of selfishness, reveal himself to us, and increase our faith.

Notice that Peter *began* to sink as he focused on the overwhelming circumstances surrounding him. I often ponder that phrase *was beginning to sink* from Matthew 14:30 because if I jumped out of a boat I wouldn't *begin* to sink, I would *immediately* sink. As Peter's faith shrank, so did his stability. But God was gracious in that he gave Peter enough time to cry out for help before he was consumed.

Time to Cry Out

I suspect most Christian couples face sexual troubles sometime in their marriage. As much as the enemy tempts people to engage in sexual behavior before they are married, he tempts them to avoid it after—at least with each other. This can be the stormiest area of marriage and the most un–talked about. The majority of counseling I have done over the years has been with women whose husbands have been unfaithful, either with a real person or with pornography. There has been a great push in the church to help men overcome their addictions to pornography and deviant sexual activity, but women are often left behind to work through the consequences on their own.

I don't know that any man can ever understand what pornography does to his wife's psyche. The rejection alone sends her spiraling into a sea of head trash. She knows she can't compete with airbrushed beauty. She obsesses over her body, thinking if she had only been thin enough or pretty enough this would have never happened. She blames immodest women, as if the root of his problems were somehow external. Meanwhile, the man may wonder why his wife can't just forgive and get back to the sexual relationship they used to have, as if his repentance eliminates the consequences. She's broken in this area, and her husband doesn't understand he's the one who broke her.

Satan uses male infidelity as an opportunity to fill the female mind with untrue accusations. The emotional and mental energy it takes her to just get through the sexual act after any kind of infidelity is often excruciating. She feels like a prostitute. Her sexual desire shuts down until trust can be rebuilt, but she is told to "do it" anyway. She feels shamed into thinking his lust problem is somehow her responsibility to fix. But she can't fix it because lust is never satisfied—it will never be enough.

She bears the burden of having to meet her husband's needs but has a hard time viewing sex as anything other than a dirty, selfish act. It is hard for her to share her intimate self with him knowing that she could easily be replaced by a magazine centerfold or a random woman at work. To her, the most vulnerable and spiritual act has become to her husband merely entertainment with any warm body. Many women enter marriage already carrying this kind of baggage.

I cannot counsel these women to "just do it." But I can offer some steps to healing. They are simple, though not easy:

1. Cry out to Jesus: "Lord, please rescue me!"
2. Repent of your own sin.
3. Ask for supernatural love and forgiveness for your husband and a pure sexual desire.
4. Ask for the lies that you believe to be exposed so you can stop believing them.
5. Believe that the Lord will give you what you need when you need it.

Ask Peter—there is joy in jumping out of the boat. When we do, we can experience the freedom and forgiveness that comes from faith in Jesus. But the jump is scary, especially when we are hurting.

Just like he did with Peter, the Lord builds our faith by waiting for us to cry out to him before he rescues us. He promises that he will respond when we seek him: "Then you shall call, and the LORD will answer; you shall cry, and he will say, 'Here I am'" (Isaiah 58:9a) for "He will surely be gracious to you at the sound of your cry. As soon as he hears it, he answers you" (Isaiah 30:19b). Our God loves to prove to each of us that he is faithful. We will begin to sink if we try to fix our trials ourselves.

Why Did You Doubt?

I know when I'm sitting in a chair opposite a stranger who has asked to meet with me that she is beginning to sink. I know she has tried everything to fix her circumstances and has put off calling me for weeks. Reaching out for help is an act of desperation. The remedy for every person, no matter what she is going through, is to *believe* in her Savior more. My job is to sort out what lies she believes and apply the truth.

I can't make her believe, though I wish I could. The problem with any kind of counseling (Christian or secular) is that no human can change another person's heart. Secular counselors teach coping mechanisms and behavior modification. Christian counselors may teach some of those things in addition to helping you understand how God's Word applies to your circumstance, but even the best kind of biblical counselor knows that only God can change a heart. The Lord uses trials to pry our hands off what we are trusting in and put them on him. We often want God to help us *out* of our trials, but he promises to help us *through* them.

Jesus calmed the storm within the disciples' hearts *before* he calmed the storm all around them. He does this with us too. I am convinced we learn most things the hard way. He must deal with our faith before he deals with our circumstances. When Jesus asked Peter, "Why did you doubt?" the answer seems obvious: *Well, I doubted because it isn't normal for a human being to stand on top of water, especially in a tempest.* It also isn't normal for a wife to forgive her unfaithful husband and find joy in the Lord through infidelity. After all, "God is our refuge and strength, a very present help in trouble" (Psalm 46:1). The psalmist also says, "It is good for me that I was afflicted, that I might learn your statutes" (Psalm 119:71). That is the truth. Believing it is the hard part.

As Peter and Jesus walked back to the boat together and got in, the lesson was over. Jesus quickly calmed the storm, and the disciples came to the conclusion they should have come to earlier after handing out many basketfuls of loaves and fish: "And those in the boat worshiped him, saying, 'Truly you are the Son of God'" (Matthew 14:33). We should come to this same conclusion. We will make it easier on ourselves if we don't resist what the Lord is doing.

Making It Stick

- Have you ever been tempted to believe that your circumstances are too difficult for even God to figure out? Do you view difficult circumstances as punishment for sin rather than believing your punishment was taken by Jesus on the cross? What causes you to take your eyes off of Christ and put them onto your circumstances? How can you put them back on Christ?

- Jesus' disciples witnessed the miracle of feeding five thousand men plus wives and children but were unmoved because their hearts were hard (Mark 6:52). A hard heart can never see God's glory. It must be supernaturally softened by God (usually with difficult circumstances). With this in mind, think about possible reasons why Jesus refused to perform miracles in Matthew 12:38–42, Mark 8:11–12, and John 6:28–36.

Eight

FRIENDSHIP AND THE FEAR OF MAN (OR WOMAN)

Have you ever had day-after-girls'-night-out regret? You had a great time, but later start replaying some of the evening's conversations and torment yourself with things you should not have said. You resolve next time to do better, talk less, and be more godly.

Female relationships are often tricky, even in the church. They can be one of the most encouraging and enjoyable treasures this side of heaven—if only we could stop trying to control them. We desire transparency, but that desire is stifled by worry about other people's opinions. We fear we might offend someone, become offended, or say something that will be misconstrued. The tendency to gossip looms, and we are always waiting for the right moment to engage. Questions race through our minds. *Do I appear godly? Have I said too much? Too little? What must so and so think of me?*

Most women long for close friendships but shy away

from their complexity. What is the solution for the day-after-girls'-night-out regret?

Oh, No! I'm Exposed!

These problems in friendship stem from self-absorption and fear of man. Some try to manufacture an image that will not be rejected. But navigating the fickle opinions of others is an exhausting and self-centered job. At the end of the day, fake people can only have fake friendships. To have real friends, you must be willing to let people in. This is risky, though. Once you let them in, they can hurt you.

Whether we talk too much or quietly hide ourselves in the crowd, the root of our turmoil is the same. We desire to be perceived a certain way. Our sin doesn't bother us when it remains hidden, but when everyone sees it, we fret, withdraw, and justify ourselves. Many women try to avoid hurt and regret by resolving never to be vulnerable again. But the Bible gives a joyful alternative to isolation: "If we walk in the light, as he is in the light, we have fellowship with one another, and the blood of Jesus his Son purifies us from all sin" (1 John 1:7).

My closest friends are those women who enjoy deep conversations about the Lord *and* are open about their sin and struggles. With them, I am free to be the same way. I also feel most comfortable being lighthearted and laughing with these same friends. We know each other well. We love each other much and extend grace, knowing each other's weaknesses. These friendships still come upon rocky times, but biblical friendship is so rare that we cherish it when we have it. We address conflict only after self-examination shows that no pettiness or imagination is involved. We assume the best. Ultimately, confrontation is rare. But when it occurs, we do it privately with gentle humility and deep love.

Friendship Must Be Free

Expectations can kill friendships. I have met many newcomers to our church who became frustrated when friendships did not develop quickly enough. While we are a welcoming church, relationships do not form overnight. They require time and effort from both parties. In addition, not all friendships can be intimate. Intimate friendships take time to maintain. No one can manage very many and still do what God is calling her to. Sometimes this is where we get into trouble.

Friendship becomes idolatry when we move from enjoying it (at every stage) to controlling it. Friendship never blossoms when one person depends on another for happiness and validation. The only person we should become dependent upon is Christ.

My first day of fifth grade, I was seated next to a boy known for being mean. It didn't take long for him to start teasing me about my red hair. "Hey carrot-top!" he said. I could feel my face and ears turn red.

"Why don't you shut up, stupid!" came a voice from across the table. I smiled at my defender, and from that day forward she and I were best friends.

"Gina" defended me a lot. I felt safe with her. She was bigger than most of the kids in our class and feared no one. For the next five years, we did everything together. We shared a locker all through junior high. We stayed at each other's houses on the weekends, sang into our curling irons, talked about boys, and put on makeup together.

Gina was content to have just one friend—me. In

exchange for my friendship, she protected me from mean kids and went along with whatever I wanted to do. I, on the other hand, became increasingly restless. I wanted to make other friends and meet new people. Gina resisted that and hindered other girls from getting to know me. I felt trapped.

I was not mature enough to handle it well. I tried acting aloof to get her to seek other friends, but it made her even clingier. I tried to be honest with her and tell her that she was smothering me, but that hurt her feelings. I finally did what any other fifteen-year-old would do — ran away from the problem. I convinced my parents to let me switch high schools for my junior and senior years. Then, I called Gina a week before school started to let her know she would have to find a new locker mate. Our friendship dwindled after that.

I am not proud of how I handled that friendship. But trying to possess a person burdens her with an occupation she cannot fulfill. The flesh is never satisfied with human attention — it will never be enough. If you require certain actions from friends, you will be devastated when they fail to meet your expectations. If you are ruled by another's opinion, you will resent her when she doesn't affirm you. If your friendship is about being served, then you are pursuing an idol — not a friendship. Love does not suck everything to itself. It is free or it is not love.

Sometimes adult relationships don't move beyond junior-high maturity, even in the church. If we want to have biblical friendships, we must allow God to build them. We need to recognize when to let go or give space. If we pursue a friendship that is not reciprocated, we need to set that friend free from our expectations and believe the best. Maybe she doesn't have time for one more intimate friend. Perhaps she is enduring a private trial that makes it difficult for her to engage in a new friendship. For whatever reason, she hasn't made time for you. Understand that God is leading you to other friends. Give grace and let her go.

Friendships can so easily turn into idolatry, but idolatrous relationships always end in resentment because no one can fill the spot designed for God. Idolatry is worshiping the creation rather than the Creator, and our hearts often deceive us about it in human relationships. We convince ourselves that we are serving others unselfishly when we're really controlled by what they think of us. People pleasing, at its root, is not concerned with what God wants. It is all about making others like us or accept us or give us praise, and that is selfishness in disguise. This sort of idolatry leads to bondage—the bondage that makes you dependent on other people.

Fear God, Not Man

What do you do with your sin? Do you confess it to God and let him take it away, or do you hide it from people? We often fear that our sin will be discovered, but it's not God we worry about—it's other people. When we feel guilt over sin committed in public, we have a choice: we can pick up the phone and do damage control with our friends, or we can confess it privately to the Lord. Confession allows us to leave our guilt (and our reputation) at the foot of the cross. Sometimes confessing our sins to each other is necessary, but it should never take the place of confessing our sins to God.

After Adam and Eve ate the forbidden fruit in the

garden, they became racked with fear and hid from God. It's hard to say what went through Adam's mind as he watched his wife take that first bite, but one thing is certain: He chose to please her rather than God. He loved her more in that moment than he loved God. He willingly sinned and then tried to cover it up.

The fear of man taken to the extreme can make people do irrational things. I have a small television in my kitchen so that I can watch the news while I cook dinner, and this headline caught my attention one evening: "A local Christian girl murders her newborn twin sons." My heart sank. I laid down my cooking utensils and gave my full attention to the story. Somehow this young woman hid her pregnancy (with twins!) from everyone. She confessed to detectives that she did not want her parents, who were in the house with her when she gave birth, to hear the babies. So after the first one was born, she put her hand over the child's mouth and held it there until the baby fell silent and died. She did the same with the second. Then, she hid their tiny bodies in a laundry basket under some blankets. Her dad later found the bodies and called the police.

Obviously, something is not right with this twenty-five-year-old woman who was raised in a local Christian church. If I were to guess what was going on in her mind, I would bet that she did not want anyone to know she was sexually active, so she hid that sin with another sin—murder. She may have been in denial for the duration of her pregnancy. What she tried to hide from her parents, the whole city now knows.

This young woman displayed her fear of man by trying to hide the evidence of her sin from her parents. She had a greater fear of them than of the God who was present in the room when she snuffed out the life of her tiny sons. She undoubtedly felt desperate, and she is not yet beyond the compassion, hope, and forgiveness of the gospel, but in that moment, she was not controlled by fear of the Lord.

So what does it mean to *fear* the Lord? Are we to literally be scared of God? The answer is yes and no. Those who do not have a saving relationship with Jesus Christ should fear God's real, eventual punishment. Christians can have confidence that Christ bore the punishment for their sin on the cross. They don't need to fear God's eternal judgment, but they do need to understand that they may face discipline here on earth.

There is a difference between punishment and discipline. When a believer falls into a pattern of sin, God will discipline her. Discipline is meant for training—not punishment. It is painful, but it is for our good. God disciplines those he loves (Hebrews 12:6).

When we properly understand this, we no longer have to fear man. "In God, whose word I praise, in God I trust; I shall not be afraid. What can flesh do to me?" (Psalm 56:4). The answer to the psalmist's question is: *nothing*! The one who draws near to Christ is free from the opinions of people, the burden of sin, and the fear of death and punishment—she is truly free! "There is no fear in love, but perfect love casts out fear. For fear has to do with punishment, and whoever fears has not been perfected in love" (1 John 4:18).

True Accountability

Even though we are called to live in freedom (Galatians 5:1), our enemy loves to sow seeds of discord in our midst to hinder the gospel and put us in bondage to the fear of man. If he can distract us with mistreatment, we will become ineffective and divisive.

One Sunday morning, someone pulled me aside in the hallway at church. "Marci," she said, "last week you passed by me without saying hello or even looking me in the eye. I feel like you are judging me by not forgiving me."

I was flabbergasted. Months before, this person had asked my forgiveness for some hypocrisy that I had witnessed. Though I did not see the need to forgive this person because she had not sinned against me, I had given it and then forgotten about it.

Now, my thoughts raced back to the previous week. I had been preoccupied by some other issue. I was so immersed in my own thoughts that I hadn't noticed this person. While I may have needed to be confronted about my self-absorption, I certainly had not ignored her on purpose and held no grudge against her. I asked, "Did you say hello to me?" The answer was no. She had made assumptions based on my facial expression and lack of eye contact. We talked it through and cleared up the misunderstanding. I was glad to have the opportunity to correct the mistake.

I cannot blame this person as I have done the same thing to others. Reading faces without any context can lead to wrong conclusions, when the apostle Paul exhorts us to only think about things that are true (Philippians 4:8). Rather than assuming or imagining motivations and attitudes when you notice someone's troubled look, why not ask her if she is okay? If you are concerned about tension in a relationship, *ask*. This may help you fulfill Paul's command: "If possible, so far as it depends on you, live peaceably with all" (Romans 12:18). If you ask and she says there is no conflict, then you must believe her and move on.

The gospel frees us from the fear of man. It liberates us from unnecessary rules and expectations we impose on each other. There is no time for pettiness between Christians (Ephesians 4:1–3). Selfishness forces the gospel into dormancy while we squabble amongst ourselves, defending our preferences and looking out for our own reputation. True friendship must originate at the foot of the cross instead. It begins with humility and is fueled by the love that the Lord demonstrated toward us. John 15:12–13 tells us, "This is my commandment, that you love one another as I have loved you. Greater love has no one than this, that someone lay down his life for his friends." Selflessness is biblical friendship.

Making It Stick

- Spouting off—with opinions, gossip, unsolicited advice, and more—can cause a lot of trouble, much of it hidden in hurt feelings and bitter resentment. Be mindful of the psalmist who wrote, "Let the words of my mouth and the meditation of my heart be acceptable in your sight, O LORD" (Psalm 19:14). Sometimes we use this excuse: "I am the kind of person who speaks my mind. That is just who I am!" What does Galatians 5:13–15 say on the one hand about freedom and on the other about the consequences of reckless tongues among believers?

- Think about your friendships. Do you have any friends toward whom you harbor bitterness because they are not meeting your expectations? Do you think more about how you can serve them or how you want them to serve you? Are you more concerned with people's opinion of you—or God's? When you find yourself frustrated that you cannot control someone else, run to the cross and find freedom in relinquishing that desire to Christ, who is in control of all.

Nine
THE TRUTH ABOUT WOMEN AND MEN

As a young woman I believed that once I had a ring on my finger, all my fears of being alone would disappear. That belief seemed confirmed when I fell in love with my husband, because he was everything I ever wanted in a man. My happily ever after had arrived.

I've heard similar expectations from other women, and it's because relationships—especially romantic ones—are important to women. Of all the things we make into idols, most women idolize human relationships more than anything else. Even more than friendships, women worship "love." We are continually fed the lie from our culture that a romantic relationship is the key to our happily ever after.

Idolatry and Worship

The unexpected twist in this kind of worship is that once we find relationships that are safe and satisfying (the very thing we think we need to make us happy) *we fear losing them*. When we fear losing them, we try to control them even more. Fear causes us to grab hold of what we worship. That is a good thing if what we worship is God, but too often, we grab hold of human relationships instead. Ironically, human relationships can die that way — from suffocation.

Perhaps it will come as no surprise to you, then, that my fears didn't disappear when I met my husband. Instead, they became more powerful. It had taken me so long to find this man that now I feared losing him. If he was late coming home from the office, I would assume he was dead in a ditch somewhere and become an emotional wreck.

This was not good for our marriage. I wanted to keep tabs on him wherever he went, and it made him feel like I was his mother rather than his wife. Once we had children, my fears multiplied. It's a full-time job just keeping preschoolers alive, and I became an overprotective, controlling mom. All of this was my effort to avoid losing people whom I loved.

In those early years of our marriage, I spent a lot of time alone as my husband got his career off the ground. And I learned, quite by accident, to draw near to the Lord. This was the benefit of the ladies' Bible study at church. We always had lessons to complete, and I wanted to be prepared. I looked forward to the fellowship and, quite honestly, the free childcare. I found comfort from God's Word and the other women. As his truth grew within me, my fears had less hold on me. I began to consciously believe that he would give me the grace to go through whatever was in my future. I could leave my worry for my loved ones at the foot of the cross.

Manipulation Versus Self-Sacrifice

What do you do to get what you think you need from your man? The "Mars and Venus" writer introduced us to our internal differences as men and women. He proposed that if we really understood what the opposite sex needed, each party would happily fulfill that need. One heading in his book reads: "How to get the support you need from your spouse with minimal sacrifice."

So, if we *understand* the best thing to do in a given situation, then follow-through will just happen? Really? If that were true, we would all be at our ideal body weight all the time. We know what it takes, but in the real moments throughout our day, we don't *want* to follow through. We don't *want* to deny ourselves.

It is helpful to understand how the opposite sex thinks, since understanding can fuel forgiveness and compassion. But the main problem in marriages is not that we don't understand what the other person needs: it's that we don't want to give it. Our sin is the problem. When two sinners are brought together, a mountain of sin lies between them. But the blindness they have toward their own sin—and the clarity they have about their partner's sin—complicates the struggle.

Lies and Expectations

I recently rented a popular chick flick to see what all the excitement was about among tween girls. It's about a vampire who falls in love with a mortal. This handsome and mysterious vampire is tormented in the presence of his mortal muse. He longs to drink her blood, which would kill her, but his desire to ravage her is controlled by his "love." He is willing to sacrifice his own desires and remain in agony just to be in her presence.

I don't even know where to begin. This movie is like porn for women. Many of us have fantasized about receiving this kind of admiration: we want to believe that there is some incredibly gorgeous man out there willing to sacrifice himself and live in torment just to be with us. But in this case, we have not just any woman, but a particularly troubled and moody one. The more emotional she is, the more he desires her. Nothing is required of her except to allow him the privilege of admiring her beauty and listening to her fears. True love drives him to protect her from his own kind. He forfeits his own happiness to serve her night and day.

This movie portrays a sexually charged, perverted version of unconditional love—what some women seek but will not find in a real man. This is a classic and raw satanic lie to women—that we are empowered by our sexuality, and that we can purchase true love with it. But it is slavery in disguise. Once we attach this fantasy to a man, he is on a course toward certain failure. He could never live up to the imagined vision even as we might work tirelessly to prove (to ourselves and others) that we are worthy of this kind of attention. We will do anything to find it. We exercise. We diet. We clothe ourselves with the latest baubles. We work hard to become "good women" worthy of love. We shackle ourselves to the world's ideal. However "good" we look—that is how "good" we are.

When you add to this the lies that men believe (and *their* version of pornography), it is no wonder disillusionment in marriage is so prevalent. Both parties head into marriage with thoughts about how *they* will be served. What a rude awakening to our sinful flesh when the gospel bids us come and serve, give and die.

Relationships, Hollywood Style

It's really no wonder that so many young women ask how I knew my husband was "the one." Hollywood says happy marriage is just a matter of making sure you find "the right one." If things don't work out, keep looking and start over with someone new. Surely he's out there somewhere. We see Hollywood's poor track record for long-lasting relationships, yet we continue to believe its lies.

On the other hand, though, single Christian women can hardly enjoy getting to know a single man without interviewing him for marriage. They want to avoid any kind of suffering in marriage, so boyfriends get disqualified when it turns out they are not Jesus. We must be wise when we choose our mates, but we must also be honest: no one can control the future, and no one can avoid suffering in marriage. Dying to yourself is painful no matter who it's with. Who bothers anymore to ask the Lord to lead her to the right man? Even those who do must fight to actually *let* him (James 4:2–3). Resting in faith and surrendering control is sometimes the hardest thing for Christian women to do.

This Isn't the Way It Was Supposed to Be

The idea of a "happy marriage" was invented not by Hollywood but by God, and it's God who renewed our hope for it when he gave us the gospel. In the beginning, God gave Adam a wife to bring him joy. Marital bliss was defined in the garden but lost in the fall. Part of Eve's curse was that she would desire to possess her husband, who would dominate her instead. It didn't take long for marriages to fall to abuse, neglect, male cruelty, and female rebellion. Too few women throughout history have had any real concept of romance. Too few men have known what loving companions their wives could be.

The gospel showed up and undid what sin and selfishness had done to marriage. From the seed of joy stemming from forgiveness in Christ, sacrificial love blossomed. When the apostles preached on biblical marriage, men must have been shocked by the command to love their wives and be monogamous. Being friends with your wife was unheard of. As the gospel transformed individuals, it inevitably transformed marriages. The Christian faith pushes forth the possibility of a fulfilling marriage through selfless love. But the world always steps in with its lies and redefines the path for getting there.

"Jean" is a recovering addict in her sixties. She's had three failed marriages and has been living in rehab institutions for the past two years. I teach a Bible study where she currently resides. She's politely quiet when I talk about the power of the gospel to her, but I can feel her disagreement.

"I know I can sort things out if I just have some time to work it out in my mind," she says, but she has little compassion for others. Once, she criticized the younger addicts in the house: "They didn't wash the dishes correctly, and I told them so! What is wrong with them? I can't imagine anyone messing up her life in her twenties. I was married and had a baby when I was in my twenties."

"My life was a complete ruin by the time I was twenty-one," I responded. "Only the gospel can transform anyone at any age."

She was quiet. "Well, I tell you what. I'm not giving up on love," she said. "I know I can make marriage work next time."

This time, I was quiet. I marveled at the ability of the human heart to believe lies about itself and yet see others' shortcomings so clearly. How determined it is to demand love and respect from others, yet angrily withhold the same from them. Jean believes that given enough time, she could figure out how to manipulate the right man into giving her what she thinks she needs. While stubbornly holding to her belief in human love, she rejects the offer of unconditional love and forgiveness the Lord has offered her countless times. What is her great sin? Drug addiction? Divorce? No, it is unbelief.

The Lord alone can heal women like Jean, and he wants to do so, but she refuses his kind of healing. "I would redeem them, but they speak lies against me. They do not cry to me from the heart, but they wail upon their beds" (Hosea 7:13b–14a). Most women would rather "wail upon their beds" trying to control their own destinies than cry out to God for help.

Why do we put our hope for happiness in something that has never satisfied before and can never satisfy? Women cannot *make* men love them. So much marital conflict comes out of a demand to be loved, respected, or served. Impatience is the insanity that continues to demand the same thing in the same way even though we continually receive the opposite. Boil it all down, and we see a flat refusal to suffer.

Suffering in Marriage

I have watched women submit to the call of suffering in their marriages for the sake of the gospel (1 Peter 2:21). I've watched others refuse and walk away. The ones who persevere with the Lord discover that somehow giving up the demand to be loved sets us free to pursue loftier goals.

First Peter 3 is written to women suffering in their marriages. Peter encourages wives to do in their marriages what Christ did for them—to suffer for the sake of another (1 Peter 3:1). Christ did not retaliate. He made no threats. Instead, he "continued entrusting himself to him who judges justly" (1 Peter 2:23). Peter's instructions rail against every natural inclination a woman possesses. We think we must keep talking until we are understood; these verses say a husband may be won over without words. We think he will respond to criticism and shame tactics; these verses say you will reach him with pure and reverent behavior. We think we can woo him with outward beauty; these verses say beauty should come from the inner self.

When we bring our neediness to Christ, he gives the peace and love we have been seeking from our husbands. Then, we can love our husbands well. We can talk to the Lord as much as we want without losing his attention. He can absorb all of our emotions and steady us with his peace: "You keep him in perfect peace whose mind is stayed on you, because he trusts in you" (Isaiah 26:3).

Confessions of a Bible Teacher

Christians do not outgrow the gospel. They don't achieve a level of righteousness and then write how-to books to help the folks who haven't figured it out yet. We never get beyond needy.

I was asked to teach a series on the power of the gospel in the various areas of a woman's life. When the time came to teach on marriage, my own marriage was in conflict. For months, every struggle we had had in our nearly twenty-year marriage had come to a climax and remained unresolved. Imagine my desire to fix this quickly before I had to stand before a group and teach about the power of the gospel in marriage!

It wasn't for a lack of trying that our impasse remained. My husband and I sought the Lord individually and together more during that time than we had in our entire marriage. Both of us confessed our sin (at least the sin we knew about) openly to the Lord, to each other, and even to other people as needed. We believed that given enough time and conversation, we could fix it. Every time the subject came up, though, resolve seemed cloudy and just out of reach. Whenever the subject did not come up, our hearts became heavy bags of wet sand weighed down with small talk. We avoided eye contact for fear of what we might find if we looked too closely. Every day, we asked the Lord for enough strength for that day to fulfill our duties…and we waited.

As I approached that time of teaching about marriage, I prayed for wisdom about how I could possibly teach on this subject, and I suddenly realized that I needed to apply the gospel to my own marriage. Turns out, this was exactly the right time to teach and write about marriage. It is humbling to share these personal matters, but I hope doing so means that every chapter in this book will ring loudly with the message to stop *doing* stuff and start *believing* the gospel more. Trials that are confusing and impossible to figure out should not take us by surprise.

Rather, they should lead us to the cross through the wake of failed self-help methods, shallow advice, and every tactic we use to escape suffering.

The Lord required me to trust that the solution was cloudy for a reason. In the meantime, he revealed hidden sin in my heart—things that make me hard to lead. He revealed sin in my husband's heart—things that make him hard to follow. During times like this, the wealth of Scripture rushes in to support and comfort us. Our weakness forces us to depend on his strength. Staring at each other with tear-stained faces, my husband and I clung to this truth.

The "obedience of faith" (Romans 1:5) is a willing acceptance of the Scripture, even when human wisdom says the opposite. The gospel is not about doing better or requiring our spouse to do better. Letting perseverance have its work means humbling ourselves and submitting to whatever trial the Lord brings. The sooner we take our expectations of marriage to the cross, the sooner we will be free from the vortex of unfulfilled human ideals.

A Not-So-Rare Extreme

Most Christian women wrestle with common frustrations and struggles in marriage. But occasionally I encounter women who are suffering in their marriages due to on-going verbal, mental, sexual, or physical abuse.

Usually a wife in this situation truly loves her husband and worries *he* will get hurt. She helps him cover his sin, therefore enabling him to continue in it. She may have a secret hope that a godly man will take notice, carefully befriend her husband, and love him into changed behavior without having to know about (or directly address) his sin. Her expectations of this scenario grow and spill onto those around her.

It is biblical for younger women to seek counsel from older women. But if you suffer from real abuse, you must turn to the male leadership of the church for help. Likewise, if you learn of such a situation in your church, you must encourage that wife to seek counsel from the church leadership and perhaps go with her to help her do so. It will probably be hard for her to trust men. She cannot even begin to think about telling them what goes on inside her home. She knows she will pay a heavy price for bringing someone in from the outside. Her husband controls her with anger, and he depends upon secrecy to keep things that way. It is for this type of situation the following passage was given:

> If you brother sins against you, go and tell him his fault, between you and him alone. If he listens to you, you have gained your brother. But if he does not listen, take one or two others along with you, that every charge may be established by the evidence of two or three witnesses. (Matthew 18:15–16)

Along with our church leaders, God also ordains legal authorities to help us when the situation warrants it. Romans 13:1–5 tells us that these officials are servants for our good, and Christians should not be slow to call upon them when needed.

Any wife in an abusive situation will be terrified at this advice, but that is where faith comes in. She will need to walk by faith and not by sight, praying fervently through each day. There's a right and a wrong way to go about this. Giving bits and pieces of information to different people will not biblically expose the sin: it will be mistaken for slander rather than a cry for help, increasing the confusing nature of this kind of trial. As an act of faith in what Matthew 18 prescribes, she should present her situation to one or two of the elders in her church. She needs to give the full story — including her own sin and exactly what she is afraid of.

Each situation has its own unique set of circumstances that cannot be addressed here. The bottom line is that we are not meant to walk the Christian life alone. No matter how much you suffer in your marriage, drawing near to Christ will make you less needy. As you learn to abide in Christ, you will not require your husband to fulfill all your needs (which he cannot do anyway), and you will cease to believe the lie that he can. When Christ fills your cup to overflowing, then the quality of your marriage will not define the happiness or unhappiness of your day.

You don't need lists of stuff to *do* to improve your marriage. Instead, do just one thing: trust your God. Give up your manipulation and draw near to Christ in your weakness. Receive his strength. Watch him work. Worship him: "True worshipers will worship the Father in spirit and truth, for the Father is seeking such people to worship him" (John 4:23).

Making It Stick

- Have you ever believed that you could find your "happily ever after" in a romantic relationship? Do you fear never finding "the right one"? If you have found "the right one," do you fear losing him? Do you believe the lie that you accidentally married "the wrong one" and that there is a "right one" you missed out on?

- We read in 1 Peter 3:5 of "holy women who hoped in God," like Abraham's wife Sarah. Read Genesis 20 and think about how Sarah entrusted herself to God even when her husband didn't. How did God show himself faithful to her even when her husband failed her?

Ten
ABIDING IN HUMILITY

As children, many of us fantasized about our toys coming to life. Maybe this is why so many movies seem based on this premise: the toys show complete loyalty and love to their owner, and their job is to bring him happiness. In the movies, toys embrace their job wholeheartedly.

Suppose as a kid you had the power to bring your toys to life. Imagine how lovingly you would expect them to respond to you, grateful that you brought them to life and willing to trust that you would love them and take care of them. Their greatest joy would surely be in the fact that you chose them and played with them.

Then one day imagine that you found them fighting with one another. Barbie and Ken moved to opposite sides of the dream house. G. I. Joe un-stuffed all the teddy bears just for fun. Even your favorite doll, Mrs. Beasley, behind those square glasses, turned into a bitter rabble-rouser. Chaos took over your room. Soon your toys were killing each other. They stopped talking to you and ignored your pleas for them to stop. Not only did they not want to play with you anymore, they wanted nothing to do with you.

What would you do? Would you not have the right to gather them in a garbage bag and start over with new toys? After all, they are your toys. You might think twice before bringing any more toys to life. You would never consider putting on plastic flesh and becoming one of them in order to help them. You definitely would not let them kill *you*.

This illustration has many flaws. We can't even begin to put ourselves "in God's shoes." But it does illustrate something of the incomprehensible humility and love it took for Jesus to even consider coming to walk among us.

The Humility of the Incarnation

Every year we celebrate the humility of Christ at Christmas—or do we? I sometimes wonder if the Christmas story has become so familiar we've exchanged its true impact for cheap sentimentality. We sugarcoat the unsanitary conditions and cruelty of our Savior's first night for pictures of quaint stables on calm snowy nights. Maybe that's the only way we can cope with the unsettling injustice of it all. God came to us, but we left him out in the cold and filth with the animals.

We sing about angels and shepherds swooning over a child sleeping peacefully on a cozy bed of hay. But the reality is, the angels and the lowlifes of society were the only locals who recognized him. The Savior was rejected by his own people from day one, and the crude nature of his birth proves that. Even in his infancy, he suffered. The reputation of being an illegitimate child followed him throughout his life. The most astonishing thing is that he chose to come to us this way.

Of all the times of the year we should spend time in reflection—thinking and meditating on the incarnation—this is it. But most of us instead degenerate during the Christmas season into a mad rush of self-indulgence, expectations, and busyness. Regular schedules get shelved in early November so Christmas traditions can take center stage.

As mothers, it is our responsibility to make sure our children have a "good Christmas." In our culture, that means *stuff*. Usually, by the end of the season, the children are fighting over big plastic toys. The adults, in a more subtle fashion, struggle with dissatisfaction about how *their* Christmas turned out. For myself, I am relieved to put away the tinsel and return to my close walk with the Lord—vowing not to get so far away from him next year.

Gift giving at Christmas started as a remembrance of the greatest gift of all time. It began with God, who forged a plan that no man could imagine because it is so contrary to human nature. The plan was this: God would humble himself in order to save prideful man.

A Humble God?

Adam and Eve enjoyed perfect fellowship with God and one another until Satan convinced Eve that God was holding out on her. It was an attractive thought to "be like God, knowing good and evil" (Genesis 3:5). If she could be like God, she would no longer need God. Human pride was born that day. The way to defeat it was with divine humility.

I minored in art history in college, especially studying

images that various people groups have crafted for the purpose of worship. It is an extraordinary phenomenon to observe from a Christian vantage point. People all over the world and throughout history have a shared need to worship something. Since certain things like weather, life, death, and illness were out of their control, they figured someone needed to be appeased. They created gods and entire religious systems to earn favor with a deity they knew must exist. Not coincidentally, the gods they made all possessed some wickedness that had to be pacified. If you were to investigate all the world's religions throughout history, you would find only one humble deity—Jesus the Messiah. In the human mind, humility and power do not go together, but in the mind of God, they do.

Philippians 2 chronicles the descent of the Lord Jesus Christ "who, though he was in the form of God, did not count equality with God a thing to be grasped, but… humbled himself by becoming obedient to the point of death, even death on a cross" (Philippians 2:6–8). With all the sermons that could be preached from these verses about the deity of Christ, one striking message clangs loudly against our human wisdom—God humbled himself! And Paul instructs us to have the same mind that Jesus had (Philippians 2:5). May God help us to direct our thoughts and emotions toward truth so that our attitudes will willingly yield.

Bait and Switch

One evening at a baby shower, an acquaintance and fellow church member asked if I would like to have lunch with her. I happily agreed. The following week we sat in a girlie-type restaurant eating great food and enjoying our conversation. When the check arrived, we each plopped down a credit card. As I was gathering my things to leave, my lunch partner suddenly changed her tone.

"Marci, I wanted to tell you that I have stopped attending Bible study, and so have three other women." I could feel my face flush. I knew this tone well, but at this moment, it had caught me off guard. *Don't be defensive, Marci. Don't be defensive*, I said to myself.

"We all feel like you come across as angry when you teach. I feel like you preach more than teach, and none of us feel like coming anymore," she said. I wanted to ask her what the difference was between "preaching" and "teaching" and what I should change in order to turn one into the other, but I remained quiet.

The problem with trying not to be defensive is that there is no protection against words stabbing your unguarded heart. It pained me to hear her words, but I had to sit there as she elaborated on my failures. My eyes overflowed with tears. I tried to blink them away so she wouldn't see I was hurt, but there was no hiding it. I asked her to tell me who the other women were so I wouldn't look around church trying to guess the three mystery dissenters. She wouldn't say.

I reminded her that I was only one of several rotating teachers. Did she feel the same way about them? She did not. I apologized and told her I would seek accountability in this area. She seemed unmoved and cold—maybe even a little smug.

When the waitress brought back our receipts, her tone changed again. "This was so much fun," she said. "We should do this once a month. I know of a great artsy restaurant we should try next month."

I didn't say it out loud, but in my heart, I thought, *I will never have lunch with you again.*

When I got home, I was devastated. It didn't help that I had to teach Bible study that same evening. I don't know why I took her criticism so hard—I guess because it was unexpected. I can usually tell when someone has an agenda. This was a bait and switch. I begged the Lord to help me get through this one last Bible study, and then I would reevaluate if I should be teaching at all.

That evening, with fear and trembling, I taught from the book of Romans. My emotions were so raw I felt I had been stripped naked and pushed to the front of the room. When I finished the closing prayer, I looked up. I understood what the faces of the women staring back at me were expressing. I was feeling the same thing. I don't know what happened that night, but it was powerful— even I could see that. Partly because I knew that power didn't come from me. I wasn't exhilarated like I had been in the past when I could tell that God had shown up. I was still fragile, but in that moment I understood that it was *necessary* for me to be stripped for that power to be unleashed.

Paul shared in 2 Corinthians that his thorn in the flesh was given to him to keep him from becoming conceited. "For the sake of Christ, I am content with weaknesses, insults, hardships, persecutions, and calamities. For when I am weak, then I am strong" (2 Corinthians 12:10). If Paul could delight in his very real persecutions, I could get over myself and delight in getting my feelings hurt every now and then. I thought, *Maybe I will have lunch with her once a month, or maybe once a week.*

Conflicts like this are a regular occurrence in my life.

I don't like drama, but I have come to see it as necessary to keep me dependent on Christ and not on the gifts he has given me. I don't have the power to soften a hard heart—that power comes only from God's Word and the Holy Spirit. Sometimes *my* heart is the thing that needs softening. Sometimes the women I spend the most time pouring my life into end up being the most resentful toward me. I recognize that I am not to gather followers unto myself so they become dependent on me, but I am to lead people to follow Christ.

The Power of Restraint

One of the greatest works the Holy Spirit has to do in me on a regular basis is to bridle my tongue when I'm angry or hurt. In my natural state, my personality can bulldoze almost anyone. But Jesus never exerted his power for selfish reasons. He submitted himself to the Father's will in everything.

Jesus's whole life was plagued by those who mocked him and hated him. At any time, Jesus had the power to kill an entire multitude with a word. He healed people from blindness; he just as easily could have afflicted others with blindness or any other malady. If we had this power at our disposal, would we be able to restrain ourselves from using it for our own purposes? I am quite sure I would be surrounded by blind people begging me for a reversal.

Think about the restraint Jesus maintained through-out his whole life—suffering unjustly at the hands of evil men. He had a greater purpose than living for his own happiness—he was here to die.

Can You See It?

There's a massive painting in The Dali Museum in St. Petersburg, Florida—an impressive thirty-by-twenty-foot landscape of a woman from behind (nude, of course) looking out at a valley from a veranda. It's one of Salvador Dali's technical masterpieces. The details are meticulous. What's more impressive, however, is what happens to those details when you step back fifty feet. When viewed from a distance, the woman disappears into a larger picture; a portrait of President Abraham Lincoln. The artistry blows my mind.

Why would Dali want to make a portrait of President Lincoln from a nude woman standing on a veranda? Who knows? But that's not the point. The point is that things are not always as they appear.

So it is with our God. His supernatural power comes through a very unexpected source—one that is hard to see because of our pride. God administers his power only through human weakness. So we need to step back and examine what our activities say about our faith: are we trusting in ourselves or God? Christian activity is often blindly fueled by human strength—and therefore is powerless.

When it comes to the gospel, perspective is everything. I can easily default to what I grew up believing—that I can make myself better. It's the same individualistic lie the world promotes: do better, discipline yourself more, choose your own destiny, be somebody. But the gospel is a gift given to sinners who humble themselves before an almighty God, surrender to his plan, and gratefully receive the sacrifice he made on the cross to pay for their sins. It doesn't demand the spotlight—it doesn't demand anything.

One of the most time-consuming lessons the Lord teaches his children is to humble themselves, patiently trust him, and stop striving in their own strength and wisdom to achieve things he isn't even calling them to. We need to step way back and look at what our God is really doing.

The Power of God

When we think of supernatural power, we might imagine moving objects with our minds or performing miraculous healings in front of masses of people. Perhaps you think of Acts 2 where the Holy Spirit descended in a violent wind and landed as tongues of fire on the believers. That's the kind of power we want.

Somehow, we are less interested in the kind of power that puts to death our selfish ambition. But that is exactly what we see at work in Acts 2. Those believers lived by faith, loving each other with reckless abandon. They had no concern for their own lives. The same Holy Spirit empowers believers today, but we tend to get preoccupied with healing bodies, making a name for ourselves, and mystical signs. We have ceased to be amazed at the miracle of a repentant sinner.

What about power over sin? If I ask myself what I hate more—my own sin or my neighbor's—I would have to answer my neighbor's, hands down. If only I could see my sin as clearly as I can see that of others! If only I could defend others as easily as I defend myself! Humility comes through seeing my sin clearly, hating it more than anyone else's, and then repenting of it and believing the Lord has taken away its guilt and will give me fresh grace and power to resist its temptations.

The concept of humility is easy to understand. We don't need a theologian to spell it out. But it is impossible to apply without abiding in Christ. When we are not abiding in him, we become selfish in our marriages, in the church, and in the world. We try unsuccessfully to control our circumstances, the people around us, and our own behavior rather than surrendering to the Lord and trusting in his sovereign control.

Galatians 5:16–18 encourages us to be stabilized by the Spirit (another way to think about remaining connected to the vine) so that we can resist our sinful desires and remain in joyful fellowship:

> But I say, walk by the Spirit, and you will not gratify the desires of the flesh. For the desires of the flesh are against the Spirit, and the desires of the Spirit are against the flesh, for these are opposed to each other, to keep you from doing the things you want to do. But if you are led by the Spirit, you are not under law.

The Lord had every right to destroy mankind at the first sign of rebellion. Instead he humbled himself so we could be lifted up. Jesus could have arrived in Jerusalem in all his glory. But because of his mercy, he clothed himself in flesh and revealed his deity through miracles. How did others respond? They killed him as he willingly yielded. The power that came from that kind of humility brought about redemption for mankind. There is power in our lives as well when we humble ourselves under God's mighty hand and entrust him to lift us up in due time (1 Peter 5:6).

It is difficult to talk about what it means to abide in

Christ without trying to define it with activity. Christ *finished* the work of redemption on the cross. That's what he meant when he said: "It is finished" (John 19:30). Resting in that truth and actually believing it is sometimes the Christian's greatest struggle. It seems too good to be true. You must experience it to understand it, and I cannot give you that experience. But I can encourage you and tell you that the Lord is faithful to teach you what it means to abide in him. Your response, daughter of God, is to believe.

Making It Stick

- The crowd mocked Jesus as he hung on the cross, saying, "If you are the King of the Jews, save yourself!" (Luke 23:37). The truth is he could have saved himself — but at great expense, for he could not then have saved others. The power to save us came through Christ's willingness to *not* save himself. In what areas of your life are lacking power because you are busy self-saving rather than yielding to the power of abiding in humility?

- Jesus said in Matthew 16:24–25, "If anyone would come after me, let him deny himself and take up his cross and follow me. For whoever would save his life will lose it, but whoever loses his life for my sake will find it." Examine your relationships. Is there anyone you love or seek approval from more than Christ? Do you need to humble yourself in any of your relationships now? Do you need to forgive, ask for forgiveness, or set anyone free from your expectations?

Endnotes

1. In this book, whenever I write about an individual or organization in a way that can be seen as uncomplimentary or overly personal, please know that names (if any) and identifying details have been changed.
2. Andrew Murray, *Abide in Christ* (Whitaker, 1979), 28–29
3. C. S. Lewis, *Mere Christianity* (Harper Collins, 2001), 136-137
4. Brother Lawrence, *The Practice of the Presence of God*, (Spire, 1969), 58

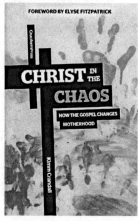

Christ in the Chaos
How the Gospel Changes Motherhood

by Kimm Crandall

MOMS: Stop comparing yourself to others. Stop striving to meet false expectations. Stop thinking your performance dictates your worth.

Look to the gospel for rest, joy, sufficiency, identity, and motivation.

"Although Kimm Crandall's message would revive any soul longing for the breath of the gospel of grace, I am especially eager to recommend this book to that heart who strives to know God and to make him known to the little ones who call her 'Momma.' Kimm is a candid and gracious fellow sojourner, faithfully pointing to God's immeasurable steadfast love and grace in the midst of our mess."
> *Lauren Chandler, wife of Matt Chandler (pastor of The Village Church), mother of three, writer, singer, and speaker*

"What an amazingly wild and wise, disruptive and delighting, freeing and focusing book. Kimm's book is for every parent willing to take the stewardship of children and the riches of the gospel seriously. This is one of the most helpful and encouraging books on parenting I've read in the past twenty years. This will be a book you will want to give to parents, to-be parents, and grandparents."
> *Scotty Smith, author; Founding Pastor, Christ Community Church*

"Kimm Crandall has discovered that chaos can be the perfect context in which to experience God's liberating grace. She is a wise, practical, gospel-drenched guide for anyone navigating through the wearisome terrain of parenting."
> *Tullian Tchividjian, author; Pastor, Coral Ridge Presbyterian Church*

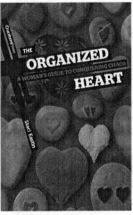

The Organized Heart
A Woman's Guide to Conquering
Chaos

by Staci Eastin

**Disorganized?
You don't need more rules, the
latest technique, or a new gadget.**

**This book will show you a different,
better way. A way grounded in the
grace of God.**

"Staci Eastin packs a gracious punch, full of insights about our
disorganized hearts and lives, immediately followed by the balm of
gospel-shaped hopes. This book is ideal for accountability partners
and small groups."

> *Carolyn McCulley, blogger, filmmaker, author of* Radical Wom-
> anhood *and* Did I Kiss Marriage Goodbye?

"Unless we understand the spiritual dimension of productivity, our
techniques will ultimately backfire. Find that dimension here. Encouraging and uplifting rather than guilt-driven, this book can help
women who want to be more organized but know that adding a new
method is not enough."

> *Matt Perman, Director of Strategy at Desiring God, blogger,
> author of the forthcoming book,* What's Best Next: How the
> Gospel Transforms the Way You Get Things Done

"Organizing a home can be an insurmountable challenge for a woman. The Organized Heart makes a unique connection between idols
of the heart and the ability to run a well-managed home. This is not
a how-to. Eastin looks at sin as the root problem of disorganization.
She offers a fresh new approach and one I recommend, especially to
those of us who have tried all the other self-help models and failed."

> *Aileen Challies, mom of three, and wife of blogger, author, and
> pastor Tim Challies*

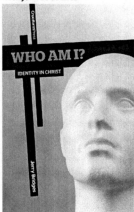

Who Am I?
Identity in Christ

by Jerry Bridges

Jerry Bridges unpacks Scripture to give the Christian eight clear, simple, interlocking answers to one of the most essential questions of life.

"Jerry Bridges' gift for simple but deep spiritual communication is fully displayed in this warm-hearted, biblical spelling out of the Christian's true identity in Christ."

>   *J. I. Packer, Theological Editor,* **ESV Study Bible;** *author,*
>   **Knowing God, A Quest for Godliness, Concise Theology**

"I know of no one better prepared than Jerry Bridges to write *Who Am I?* He is a man who knows who he is in Christ and he helps us to see succinctly and clearly who we are to be. Thank you for another gift to the Church of your wisdom and insight in this book."

>   *R.C. Sproul, founder, chairman, president, Ligonier Ministries;*
>   *executive editor,* **Tabletalk** *magazine; general editor,* **The**
>   **Reformation Study Bible**

"*Who Am I?* answers one of the most pressing questions of our time in clear gospel categories straight from the Bible. This little book is a great resource to ground new believers and remind all of us of what God has made us through faith in Jesus. Thank the Lord for Jerry Bridges, who continues to provide the warm, clear, and biblically balanced teaching that has made him so beloved to this generation of Christians."

>   *Richard D. Phillips, Senior Minister, Second Presbyterian*
>   *Church, Greenville, SC*

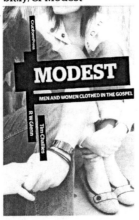

Modest

Men and Women Clothed in the Gospel

by R W Glenn, Tim Challies

Modesty is about freedom, not rules.

What you say or do or wear is not really the point. The point is your heart.

True modesty flows from a solid grasp of the gospel.

"It is so refreshing to have a book on modesty that is a useful resource and not a legalistic, culture-bound list that leaves you a bit paranoid and guilty. No, this book is different. Its counsel on modesty is not rooted in rules, but in the grace of the gospel of Jesus Christ. That grace alone is able to get at the heart of the problem of modesty, which *is* the heart. In a culture where immodesty is the accepted norm, Glenn and Challies have given us help that every Christian desperately needs."
Paul Tripp, pastor, conference speaker, and author

"How short is too short? How tight is too tight? Glenn and Challies don't say. But they do provide a thoughtful framework to help us come to a grace-based, gospel-grounded understanding of modesty that extends beyond mere clothing. They uphold a vision for modesty that's both beautiful and desirable – and not only for gals, but for guys too! This book is a great tool to help you wrestle with the practical question of what and what not to wear."
Mary A. Kassian, Author, **Girls Gone Wise**

"The authors of Modest break new ground in their treatment of this difficult subject. It is a healthy antidote to the prevailing views, which tend toward either legalism or antinomianism, by grounding the whole subject in the gospel. I heartily recommend this book."
Jerry Bridges, Author, **The Pursuit of Holiness**

Friends and Lovers
Cultivating Companionship and
Intimacy in Marriage

by Joel R. Beeke

Marriage is for God's glory and our good.

The secret?

Intimate Christian companionship.

"A book about love, marriage, and sex from Joel Beeke that is surprisingly candid yet without a trace of smuttiness. Fresh and refreshingly straightforward, this is the best book of its kind."

Derek W H Thomas, Visiting Professor, Reformed Theo. Sem.

"Marriage is hard work. And wonderful. And sometimes, it's both at the same time. *Friends and Lovers* is like a personal mentoring session on marriage with a man whose heart is devoted to seeing Christ honored in how we love each other as husbands and wives. It's full of practical wisdom and grace. A delight."

Bob Lepine, Co-Host, FamilyLife Today

"By laying the theological, emotional, social, and spiritual foundations of marriage before heading to the bedroom, Joel Beeke provides a healthy corrective to the excessive and obsessive sex-focus of our generation and even of some pastors. But, thankfully, he also goes on to provide wise, practical, down-to-earth direction for couples wanting to discover or recover physical intimacy that will both satisfy themselves and honor God."

Dr. David Murray, Professor, Puritan Reformed Theo. Sem.

"There is no better book than this to renew the affection of happy marriage."

Geoffrey Thomas, Pastor, Alfred Place Baptist Church, Wales

bit.ly/JoyStudy   bit.ly/FaithStudy

Inductive Bible studies for women by Keri Folmar
endorsed by...

Kathleen Nielson is author of the *Living Word Bible Studies*; Director of Women's Initiatives, The Gospel Coalition; and wife of Niel, who served as President of Covenant College from 2002 to 2012.

Diane Schreiner – wife of professor, author, and pastor Tom Schreiner, and mother of four grown children – has led women's Bible studies for more than 20 years.

Connie Dever is author of *The Praise Factory* children's ministry curriculum and wife of Pastor Mark Dever, President of 9 Marks Ministries

Kristie Anyabwile, holds a history degree from NC State University, and is married to Thabiti, Senior Pastor of First Baptist Church, Grand Cayman, and a Council Member for The Gospel Coalition.

Gloria Furman is a pastor's wife in the Middle East and author of *Glimpses of Grace* and *Treasuring Christ When Your Hands Are Full*.

Luma Simms is author of *Gospel Amnesia: Forgetting the Goodness of the News* and *Counterfeit Me* (forthcoming)